A Good Catch

Colin Isaac

A Good Catch

Colin Isaac

Paperback Edition First Published in the United Kingdom
in 2016 by aSys Publishing

eBook Edition First Published in the United Kingdom
in 2016 by aSys Publishing

Copyright © Colin Isaac

Colin Isaac has asserted his rights under 'the Copyright
Designs and Patents Act 1988' to be identified as
the author of this work.

All rights reserved.

No part of this book may be reproduced or transmitted in any form or by any means, electronic, mechanical, photocopying, recording, or otherwise, without prior written permission from the Author.

Disclaimer

This is a work of fiction. Names, characters, businesses, places, events and incidents are either the products of the author's imagination or used in a fictitious manner. Any resemblance to actual persons, living or dead, or actual events
is purely coincidental.

ISBN: 978-1-910757-66-6

aSys Publishing
http://www.asys-publishing.co.uk

For my wonderful daughter, Lisa

Chapter 1
CHANGES

Thomas George Bevan–known to virtually everyone in the village as "T.G."–looked up at the scoreboard and almost wept. 32 for 9. Horrendous! This was the worst performance yet–and there were only five weeks to go to the big day.

T.G. held back the tears. But there was no holding back the anger when the last wicket fell. 32 all out! The shame of it. The disgrace. And only five weeks to go.

He stormed on to the field and headed straight for the not-out batsman, the captain. The situation was serious and something had to be done quickly. There was no time to lose. Only five weeks to go.

* * *

Five weeks to go before what? The answer to that question could be given by anyone in the village. In five weeks' time Marwen Cricket Club would entertain their close rivals from the neighbouring village, Ramley. This was South Wales' cricketing equivalent of Celtic v Rangers, Labour v Conservative, Tom v Jerry.

It would be a day when only one thing would occupy the minds of the villagers of Marwen–winning the match. Most of the villagers didn't even follow cricket. But this game was different. This was not a mere cricket match. This was a matter of honour, a matter of pride. This was war!

Whatever else the cricket team did during the season, they had to pull out all the stops for this match. It was a game they dare not lose.

The 1979 fixture list hanging on the notice-board in the clubhouse attested to the importance of the Ramley match. Saturday 30 June Marwen v Ramley. These words were highlighted in red to make them stand out from the rest of the fixtures.

Saturday 30 June. In five weeks' time.

* * *

Clive Walters, the Marwen captain, saw T.G. hurrying towards him and knew what was coming. By now he was quite used to the chairman's outbursts. Not that there was any need for T.G. to say anything. It was all too evident that the team was playing badly. This was the third defeat in a row—and only three matches they had played so far this season.

No surprise therefore that the villagers of Marwen were getting worried about the team's prospects in the big game on June 30th. Clive was worrying too. After all, he was the captain.

"What the hell is going on?" T.G. came straight to the point as usual. "That's the worst display I've ever seen on a cricket pitch."

Clive was going to say something, but T.G. wasn't finished yet. "I'm telling you, Clive, there'll have to be changes. This can't go on. We've only got five weeks left before Ramley. Five weeks."

"Calm down T.G.," said the captain.

"Calm down? How the hell can I calm down after seeing that shambles. The team I captained here twenty years ago could beat your lot now. And four of my team are dead. Mind you, with the amount of movement out there today, I wouldn't be surprised if some of your team are dead too."

There was no point trying to reason with T.G. when he was in this sort of mood, so Clive said, "I'm not listening to any more of this" and walked off in the direction of the changing rooms.

T.G. followed him. "You'll have to listen to more of this. You wait until the committee meeting. You'll hear a lot more then."

Clive stopped and turned to face his team's greatest critic. "As chairman T.G., you have the right to an opinion. But it's only an opinion."

"An opinion," said the chairman, "which will be voiced—and supported—in Monday night's meeting. There are going to be changes in this team. And my opinion"—he emphasised the word—"is that those changes could even include the captaincy."

T.G. didn't give Clive a chance to reply. He charged off towards the clubhouse. Clive watched him go, then shrugged his shoulders and made his way to the changing rooms.

* * *

The captain entered the changing room to find most of his team already changed. The players were certainly no slouches when it came to drinking and they wanted to get to the clubhouse as quickly as possible.

Kevin Williams, the "Don Juan" of the team, was combing his hair for the fourth time since changing. His fair hair was always neatly in place and this was only one feature of his good looks. Although on the short side, Kevin was very proud of his body. "An athlete's body" he called it. Not an ounce of excess fat anywhere, according to him. The moustache he had recently grown made him look a little older than his twenty-six years—or, as Kevin would have it, made him look more mature and sophisticated.

Kevin himself was the first to admit that he was handsome. And he should know, the number of times he stood in front of a mirror each day. He was standing in front of a mirror when Clive came in. "Hard lines, skip," he said. "If you hadn't run out of partners, you could have got a century today."

"If he hadn't run them out, you mean," quipped one of the others, at which everyone laughed except Clive.

"This is no time to joke," said the frowning captain. "We're in a bad way, in case you haven't noticed. With only five weeks to go before Ramley. And after today's display, no-one here can be sure of playing next week, let alone in five weeks' time."

Kevin smiled. "You've been talking to T.G."

"Yes, I have," Clive replied immediately. "And he's determined to make changes."

"What changes?" sneered Kevin. "Who can he bring in to improve the team?"

"John Price's youngest lad for one," asserted the captain. "And he's only a year old. But I've seen him throw a rattle further than you managed to throw the ball today, Kev."

"O.K., boys. Cool it," said Bob Evans, who could see that the situation was in danger of becoming somewhat less than friendly.

Bob, a solicitor in his mid-twenties, was the quiet man in the team. He disliked arguments, saying that he had enough of those to contend with in his work, and he could be counted on to smooth over any rifts which developed within the club.

The only rift which gave him any difficulty was that developing between himself and his girlfriend, Carol Treharne. She hated cricket and was incensed by the fact that "Robert", as she called him, was taken from her each Saturday in order to play bat and ball with a bunch of immature drunkards who ought to know better.

Bob himself, however, enjoyed his cricket and although Carol tried various means to sidetrack him, he invariably found some way out in order to play for the team each week. And they needed him. He was the most consistent player they had. Even today he had scored 20 of the 32 runs.

They also needed someone like Bob to calm things down when tempers became heated and it was no surprise that it was Bob who had interrupted Clive and Kevin now.

Arthur Howells, the wicket-keeper and at fifty-one the oldest member of the team, then entered the discussion. "It's alright for you, Bob. They'd never drop you. But what about the rest of us? If I'm left out, I'm stuck at home with the dragon."

It was a standing joke within the club how Arthur disliked staying in with his wife. He would do anything to get out of the house—umpire youth matches, serve behind the bar, anything.

"Your place is safe too," Bob told Arthur. "Or we wouldn't have a wicket-keeper."

"According to T.G.," Arthur replied, "even with me we haven't got a wicket-keeper."

Everyone laughed, but it was an uneasy laughter now. An air of tension had crept into the room.

"And your place is safe, Clive," Bob told his captain.

"Not according to T.G.," Clive said despondently.

The others looked at each other in silence, realising now what was worrying the skipper. The silence continued as Clive took off his pads and started changing.

By now Kevin had satisfied himself that each hair was perfectly in place and had put on some more after-shave (the second time that evening), much to the annoyance of the two other players who had been subjected to an uninvited dowsing of the liquid as Kevin splashed it on. Having checked himself yet again in the mirror, Kevin turned. "Come on, boys. Cheer up. It's Saturday night."

Clive turned to face him. "And what have you got to be so cheerful about?"

Kevin headed for the door. "I told you I'd have a good score today."

"You only got two runs," said Arthur.

"Who's talking about cricket?" Kevin opened the door. "Did you see the girl they brought with them to do the scoring? Cheers, lads." And off he went.

Arthur shook his head. "I don't know how he does it."

Bob, however, was not amused. "The sooner he settles down with one girl, the better off he'll be."

"Why should he? He's enjoying himself. Once you settle down with one girl, she starts to run your life and then you can say goodbye to enjoyment, freedom, all the pleasures of life."

"You're wrong there, Arthur. Take Carol and me. We've been going out for over two years now and she doesn't run my life."

Arthur raised his eyebrows questioningly, knowing the trouble Bob had each week getting away from Carol to play for the team. Bob was the only person in the village who failed to see how much control Carol had over him.

"Anyway, I'm thirsty," said Arthur, picking up his bag. "Let's discuss the matter over a few pints."

Bob agreed readily at first, then looked at his watch and said in a low voice, "Well, perhaps I'll just have a quick half before going."

Even Clive couldn't keep from laughing with the others at that. Bob's face turned red with embarrassment and he left as quickly as he could, with Arthur following a few paces behind. They could still hear the laughter as they made their way to the clubhouse, a separate building some twenty yards away. Poor Bob!

Poor Clive! He sat in the changing rooms for ten minutes after all the others had left, pondering the prospect of losing the captaincy. He had been captain for the last two years and thought he'd made quite a good job of it. Not so much in terms of results perhaps, though those had been fairly good overall. But in terms of creating a good team spirit he certainly had been a success. The players respected him and would do anything for him. And he for them. They knew that.

But now he had to face the possibility of losing the captaincy. And it might not end there. If he lost the captaincy, he might also lose his place in the team—and, worst of all, he might miss the Ramley game.

With such thoughts deepening his depression, Clive got up and made his way to the clubhouse. Perhaps Pat could cheer him up.

* * *

Pat Walters was standing at the bar, having just bought a pint of bitter for her husband and a dry martini for herself. She was talking to the girl who had served her—Jessica Bevan, T.G.'s daughter. Actually, Pat was listening rather than talking, because Jessica was once again on her soap-box giving the same sermon that Pat and virtually everyone else at the club had heard so often before.

Jessica was determined to play for the cricket team. It was one of her main ambitions. It had been ever since she first came down to the club with her father at the age of five. Now, fifteen years on, the ambition was undiminished—and unfulfilled. The injustice of the situation infuriated Jessica. She knew she was good enough. She showed that in the nets every Tuesday evening in the practice sessions. Yet when the team sheets were pinned up on the notice board, her name was never included.

The main stumbling block was her father. T.G. made no secret of the fact that as long as he was chairman, no woman would play for Marwen Cricket Club. To T.G. equality of the sexes was as realistic as trout-fishing in the Sahara.

His daughter, however, was nothing if not persistent. She was determined to get into the team somehow. She would help with the food, serve behind the bar, do anything that would keep her around the cricket club, in case the team was ever short and needed her to play.

Pat now had to listen to Jessica going on about the improvement her inclusion would make to the team. The two were very good friends, so Pat knew how strongly Jessica felt about this. Indeed, she sympathised with the girl's problem. But what could she do about it? Marwen Cricket Club just wasn't ready yet for a female player.

Pat saw her husband coming into the clubhouse and was glad of the excuse to get away from Jessica's latest tirade. She took the drinks to a nearby table and Clive came to sit beside her. She could see immediately that he was in low spirits. It wasn't often that Clive got depressed. In fact, he was usually the one to lift others out of their depressions. But on the few occasions when he did feel down, Pat could tell immediately without his having to say a word. The tell-tale sign was in his eyes. The blue eyes which normally sparkled and seemed to exemplify his love of life took on a sad, haunting quality which tore at Pat's heart whenever she witnessed it. It was that look which Pat could see now.

"What's the matter, love?" she asked.

"Nothing," he said and picked up his pint, downing half of it before putting the glass back down. He looked around the large main room of the clubhouse without really registering what he saw. Then he sighed. "Well, at least the food was good today.

It's nice to know one member of the Walters household can do something properly."

He was referring to the fact that Pat was in charge of the teas at the club. They had a rota system whereby players' partners took turns to prepare the teas and the drawing up of the rota was Pat's responsibility. Although she herself was listed for certain games only, Pat still came down to every home game to make sure everything ran smoothly. Anyway, she enjoyed coming to watch the cricket.

"There's no need to be like that," she told her husband. "It wasn't your fault the team lost."

Clive picked up his glass again and looked at it. "That's not how T.G. sees it. He's talking about a change of captain."

The cause of the depression now became clear to Pat. "He's talking nonsense," she said firmly. "Things will improve soon, you'll see."

As Clive started drinking the remainder of his pint, T.G. came over to the table. "Good evening, Pat," he said, putting his glass of whisky on the table. Noticeably he said nothing to Clive. "Did you see that farce out there today? Pathetic, wasn't it. If someone"–he paused, glancing at Clive–"could arrange the team half as well as you arrange the food, we wouldn't be in such a mess now."

Pat's reply was immediate. "That's not fair, T.G., and you know it. There's no comparison between the two."

"Isn't there?" T.G. asked, picking up his glass. "Food doesn't move, does it. There's one similarity straight off." Having made his point, T.G. excused himself and moved to another table, no doubt to spread gloom over proceedings there as well.

"There you are," said Clive. "You've heard it from the big man's own mouth."

"From the old man's big mouth, you mean. Anyway, he didn't say anything about the captaincy."

"You wait till the meeting on Monday night. He'll have plenty to say then."

"There's still no need to worry, love. He's only one voice on the committee. The others won't agree to a change of captain so early in the season."

"Don't be so sure," said the current captain. "There are only five weeks to go before the Ramley match. They'll want everything sorted out before then."

Pat knew how much it meant to Clive to captain the team, especially in the Ramley matches. Surely they wouldn't take the captaincy away from him now. Seeds of doubt started to take root in her mind.

"Drink up," she said. "Let's get out of here, get a bottle of wine and take it home."

"No," said Clive resolutely. "Leave here, yes. But we're not going home. We'll go down to the Red Lion and have a drink there. Well, not *a* drink. Lots of drinks. As many as it takes for me to forget all about this cricket team and its chairman."

Pat hoped he wouldn't go that far. She didn't mind the Red Lion, though they didn't go there often. Usually they went to the Cross Inn or the cricket club. In fact, Pat had some happy memories of the Red Lion. It was there they went their first evening in Marwen after moving from Swansea twelve years ago. She remembered how that night Clive carried her over the threshold. How romantic he could be at times!

She now watched him finish off his pint. Somehow it didn't seem likely that there would be a romantic end to this particular evening. Perhaps tonight it would be her turn to carry him over the threshold.

* * *

The cricket club committee met each Monday evening at 8 o'clock in a side room in the clubhouse. There were five men on the committee: T.G., the chairman; Glyn James, the secretary; Donald Owen Cooper, the treasurer; Clive and Arthur.

Other clubs had larger committees, but Marwen Cricket Club had always prided itself on having a small number. It made arranging meetings at short notice much easier and also tended to reduce the length of the meetings. The committee was still representative of most of the different elements within the club and this system had worked well enough for the past thirty years. So why change it?

T.G. sat at the head of the table as usual. His chubby face and red cheeks gave him the appearance of an amiable farmer. Yet he hadn't worked on a farm in his life. His was the grocery store in the centre of the village and it was there he worked each day, helped by his daughter. His wife had died ten years ago.

The pint of bitter and glass of whisky near his left hand, together with the very noticeable beer belly of which he was so proud, attested to the fact that T.G. enjoyed his drink. He enjoyed cricket too, but drinking was the first priority.

Sitting to his right was Glyn James, the tall, lean, bespectacled secretary of the club, who never touched alcohol. This was strange in view of the fact that he spent so much of his time at the club. But he was quite happy to drink a pint of orange and lemonade or a glass of cranberry juice or even water. The other members had by now stopped making fun of this and had given up all efforts to get him to partake of alcohol.

Glyn was an old man in his thirties. Although only thirty-eight in terms of years, he was very much older in outlook and way of life. He was a single man, presumably because most women who shared his likes and ideas were in retirement homes.

His life revolved around the cricket club and the chapel choir. He was secretary for both. An accountant by profession, he enjoyed organising things and people. Yet, in spite of his undoubted organisational ability, he tended to panic quite easily and would envisage all sorts of problems where none existed.

He was well-liked in the village and the club and it was no secret that the smooth running of Marwen Cricket Club over the past ten years was due largely to the efforts of this young old man.

Next to Glyn sat Donald Owen Cooper, known to everyone in the club as "Doc" (because of his initials rather than his profession—he was an undertaker). Doc was one of those elderly people whose appearance and demeanour seem to exude an aura of wisdom, the sort of person one feels could put the world to rights if only given the chance. Perhaps this was due to his mop of white hair, almost matched by the pallor of his skin. Indeed, one of the standing jokes at the club was to tell Doc never to go on a skiing holiday for fear that no-one would be able to spot him in the snow.

Doc had played little cricket during his sixty years on this earth but he had followed the game avidly and admitted it was his number-one love (much to the annoyance of his wife, who currently stood at number two in the ratings). His comprehensive knowledge of cricketing matters and masterly ability to analyse the game made him ideally suited to represent Marwen at League meetings and the like.

Doc never missed a home game and he also attended most of the away games. He knew the strengths and weaknesses of the team and his opinion was well-respected.

Clive had sat silently through the first half-hour of the meeting as various administrative matters were raised and dealt with, mainly by Glyn James. Then he noticed T.G.'s face take on a sterner look and he knew the time had come to discuss the team for the coming Saturday's game at Penford.

"Right, gentlemen," said the chairman. "Now for the most important matter on the agenda. Team selection." He paused for effect. "To say that I'm horrified at the present situation would be an understatement. We've been hammered out of sight in our three matches to date and on Saturday couldn't even manage one batting point."

The others listened quietly as T.G. went on. "I don't need to remind anyone here that the match against Ramley is less than five weeks away. And I for one would dread the prospect of taking them on with our present team.

"There's a lot of pride at stake here. Our team—if you can call it that—is becoming a laughing stock both inside and outside the village. I intend to put a stop to that immediately. We have to make changes."

Glyn James reinforced the seriousness of the situation. "Another point to remember, of course, is our League position. We're now well and truly at the bottom and if we don't start winning soon, we'll lose touch completely with the teams above us."

T.G. resumed where he had left off. "The team we have isn't good enough and the players aren't working hard enough."

Doc then voiced his agreement and it became evident that the non-playing members of the committee were bent on making changes.

It was time for Clive to speak out. "I don't agree with you at all on this. There's no need for changes yet. O.K., we've made a bad start. But we've had bad starts before. We shouldn't panic just because a number of players are off form at the same time. And that's all it is. A loss of form. Once it comes back, we'll be alright. All we need to do is be patient. In time things will improve."

"In time we'll all be in the cemetery," said T.G.

Doc turned to the chairman. "But you've always said you're going to be cremated." No-one laughed, least of all T.G.

Clive continued with his defence of the team. "Once two or three of the lads start picking up, it'll spread confidence through the rest of the team and then we'll be on our way."

"Yes," T.G. said. "On our way down to the Third Division."

"We won't go down, T.G."

"You'd have been saying that if you'd been on the Titanic."

"I don't care what you say. I think we should stick with this team."

"Stick or sink?"

This two-way conversation was beginning to make the others feel a little uncomfortable. It was time for someone to intervene. The secretary made the move. "What changes have you in mind, T.G.?"

"I think we should start at the top," the chairman replied assertively. "Nothing personal, Clive, but I think we should try someone else as captain to see if he can get more out of the players."

Arthur now spoke for the first time at the meeting. "Hold on, T.G., Clive's a good skipper."

"Is he?" The chairman turned on the wicket-keeper, to whose views he would normally have listened with respect. "He hasn't

A Good Catch

won a game yet."

Arthur refused to be ruffled and continued in his normal calm tone. "The team hasn't won a game yet."

"And the captain is responsible for the team." T.G. almost spat out the words. "I've already had a word with Doc and Glyn about this and they can see my point."

Before Arthur could reply, Clive spoke. "Well, gentleman, I think I have an answer to your problem. Those here who aren't happy with my captaincy will be glad to know that I'm unavailable for the next two games."

"Why didn't you say this before?" yelled T.G., his face taking on an even redder hue than usual. He rarely got as worked up as this at meetings.

Clive smiled. "I just wanted to see to what extent the committee was behind me. I must say, I've been touched by your loyalty and support."

T.G. was obviously getting ready for another onslaught, so Glyn said quickly, "O.K. then. There's the answer to our problem. We can appoint someone as captain for the next two games and review the situation in a fortnight."

"Two games aren't enough," said T.G.

"You're quite happy to judge Clive on just three games," Arthur retorted.

Doc said that Glyn's idea was an acceptable compromise and that they should now turn to the question of who was going to captain the side for the next two weeks.

After a very brief silence T.G. suggested Arthur, who thanked the chairman for the offer, then politely declined it. T.G. reminded Arthur that there were other changes to come and that if another wicket-keeper were chosen, he would have to stay home with his wife on Saturday. Arthur accepted the captaincy.

T.G. had obviously done some homework before the meeting because he informed the committee that John Price, an ex-player, had agreed to return to help out over a short period. "It'll be good to have a tidy spin bowler in the side again," remarked the chairman.

"I agree," said Doc. "But John isn't getting any younger and he won't be particularly quick about the field, will he."

T.G.'s reply was immediate, if predictable. "In that case, he'll fit in very well."

Glyn suggested that Andy Jones, a youth team player, be given a chance. Doc pointed out that while Andy was indeed a good bowler, his batting was very weak.

"So he should fit in well too," said T.G. dryly.

After a little further discussion, it was decided to bring in John Price and Andy Jones in place of Clive and Gareth Hughes, who would now be the reserve for Saturday's game. It was agreed not to make further changes yet, but performances in Saturday's game would be scrutinised very closely.

Glyn read out the finalised team, then the meeting was ended.

Clive and Arthur were the first to leave the committee room, but they hadn't gone far before T.G. came up behind them, put an arm on Clive's shoulder and started trying to smooth the troubled waters. "No hard feelings, Clive. As I said in there, it's nothing personal. I'm just trying to get us out of this mess before it's too late."

Clive nodded silently, not really wishing to converse with a man who had gone down in his esteem so much so quickly.

"And to prove there are no hard feelings, let me buy you both a drink. The two captains together. What'll you have, boys?"

They certainly needed a drink now. T.G.'s offer to buy was a far greater shock than the change in captaincy. This was indeed a rare occurrence. Clive had been living in Marwen for twelve years and he'd never seen it happen. Arthur had been living there all his life and he'd only seen it happen twice.

"I'll have a whisky and soda," said Arthur.

"Gin and tonic for me," said Clive and as T.G. moved towards the bar, the ex-captain added, "And just to show there are no ill-feelings, why not make them doubles?"

T.G.'s chin seemed to drop a good two inches. If the look on his face was anything to go by, it would be a long time again before T.G. bought a drink for anyone other than himself.

Clive and Arthur were still laughing as they sat at a table in the corner. Then Arthur broached a subject which had been troubling him since Clive had mentioned it in the meeting "I didn't know you were unavailable for Saturday."

"Neither did I," replied Clive, who then went on to explain that he preferred saying he was unavailable to giving T.G. the chance of taking the captaincy away from him. "Anyway," he added, "it'll be a nice break."

Meanwhile T.G. was being served at the bar by his daughter. As she was getting the drinks, she asked her father if she was in the team for Saturday.

"Of course not, girl," he answered. "I've told you often enough, you'll never play for the team. I don't know why you keep asking. A cricket team is no place for a young girl."

"Why not?" she asked.

"You know why not. Cricket's a man's game. Can you imagine what it would do to the morale of the team if a woman was picked? There's little enough spirit in the side as it is. We don't want to dampen it any further."

By now Jessica had placed the drinks on the bar, one gin and tonic and two glasses of whisky. She picked up the soda syphon, but instead of adding soda to the whiskies, she pointed the syphon at her father and added soda to him instead.

"What the hell are you doing?" he yelled as he jumped back.

"I didn't want to dampen the spirit in the glasses either," she replied before slamming the syphon down and storming off to the other end of the bar.

T.G. added the soda to the drinks himself, wondering what he had done that was so wrong. Still, he had bought three doubles without having to pay a penny for them. This was quite a coup.

That's what Jessica thought too, because she was back as quick as a flash to take his money before he had lifted one glass.

* * *

Clive was miserable throughout the week. The captaincy had gone. For two weeks at least. Perhaps for good. Would he even be able to get back into the team? He doubted it. So what? He didn't mind. That's what he kept telling Pat. But he didn't really believe it. She didn't really believe it either.

On Saturday morning Clive was in a very quiet mood. By eleven o'clock he had hardly spoken a word. After breakfast he had just sat quietly in his favourite chair, smoking his pipe and reading the paper. Though for the amount that he remembered of what he had read, he might as well have smoked the paper and read the pipe.

"What shall we do this afternoon?" Pat asked him.

He thought for a moment, then said, "We could go for a run in the car. It's a nice day. How about the Black Mountain? We haven't been up there for years."

"That would be nice. As long as you don't mind."

"Why should I mind? I've got nothing else to do."

Clive went back to his paper, to a paragraph he had started to read eight times previously without once getting near completing it. This ninth attempt was to fare no better. He put down the paper, then made an announcement which took Pat completely by surprise. "I've decided to pack in the cricket. I'll tell them next week. I've finished playing for good."

Pat was unable to say anything. She merely looked at him with a stunned expression.

"Think about it," he went on. "We'd have more time together. We could go to a different place each week. We've been so tied to that cricket club, our Saturdays haven't been our own for years."

"I've never complained," Pat said.

"I know, love. But we should be able to go out and enjoy ourselves whenever we want. Once the cricket season starts we lose not just the Saturday afternoons but the evenings as well."

"Oh, it's not that bad. The way the team's playing now, we usually get away quite early."

"Don't you start. I get enough comments like that from people outside."

Pat smiled. "Sorry, dear."

They sat in silence for a few moments, each assessing the

significance of Clive's announcement. After all, he was as surprised as she was. The thought had only just come to him.

The silence was broken by the ringing of the phone. Clive was out of his chair before Pat had a chance to move. She knew why he had moved so quickly. He thought it might be someone from the club. And it was.

"Hello?...Arthur! How are things?...Yes, we've arranged to go out. We'll be leaving before long...Oh?...Have you called Gareth?...Flu? In this weather?...No, I don't think I can. Sorry...Oh?...What did T.G. say?...Did he?...Was he?...No, I don't think so, Arthur...Oh?...Are you sure?...I'll be there by twelve thirty...Goodbye, Arthur. Thanks."

Clive went back to his chair. He avoided his wife's gaze. But he could not avoid Pat's determination to enjoy herself at his expense.

"What were you saying now about packing in cricket?" she asked.

Clive shifted uneasily in his chair "Er...Yes...But they're in a bit of a mess today."

"Oh?"

"They want me to play–and to be captain. Even T.G. has agreed."

"Oh?"

"Well, I couldn't let them down, could I."

"And what about letting me down? I was looking forward to seeing the Black Mountain again."

"Oh!" Now Clive felt really uncomfortable. He hadn't considered that his wife might actually be looking forward to the afternoon's trip. He got up slowly. "I'm sorry. I'll ring Arthur back. They can get someone else."

Pat laughed. "Don't be silly. I was only joking. You go and put your kit ready. I'll see to our early lunch." Clive still looked unconvinced, so Pat added, "It's an away match, so I can still get a run in the car. I'll come with you."

* * *

As it turned out, they still got to see the Black Mountain. The game was over by five past six. Marwen were all out for 61 runs in reply to Penford's 95 all out.

Needless to say, T.G. was furious that the team had lost again. He cornered Clive as the captain was going to his car after changing. "Four weeks to go and we still can't get into three figures."

Clive tried to soothe the chairman, who was again turning an unhealthy shade of red. "Don't worry about it, T.G. Things are improving. We've nearly doubled last weeks score. If we do the same next week and in the following weeks, we'll be in top form for the Ramley game."

"Don't you talk about next week. Nor anyone else in the team. I'm telling you, Clive, there are going to be changes. I'm not..."

"Yes, T.G.," Clive interrupted. "Quite right. But I can't stop now. Leave it till Monday night." Then he got into the car and smiled at Pat, who was already there.

"Where do you think you're going?" the chairman thundered.

Clive started the engine. "The Black Mountain," he said and eased the car away.

"Why don't you take the rest of the team with you?" T.G. yelled after them. "And leave them up there."

Clive put his arm out of the window and waved. Again he smiled at Pat. And why not? Things were improving–and there were still four more weeks to go.

Chapter 2

EGGSTRAORDINARY

Clive kept his team place and the captaincy for the following week's home game with Temway. But as things turned out, he would never come closer to losing the captaincy, his team place and his club membership all at once than he did that day. And all because the normally sedate Marwen skipper let his hair well and truly down in a birthday celebration he would never forget.

It was his forty-fifth birthday and, with the team playing at home, he was looking forward to having a good time at the club in the evening.

Had he and Pat had children, they would have celebrated the occasion in some other way. But Pat was unable to have children and, although they had talked about adoption, they had never taken the matter very far. Still, they had a very happy marriage. They had been married for fifteen years. As Clive said, "Fifteen not out and hoping for a half-century at least."

As he sat in bed on the Saturday morning, Clive could hear Pat downstairs making the breakfast. He wondered what present she had bought him for his birthday. That was something he had always liked about Pat: she never gave any idea as to presents she had bought, she always managed to maintain the surprise element. And, though Clive had long since left childhood, he nevertheless retained a child-like love of surprises.

So what would be today's surprise? There was only one way to find out. Clive got out of bed and made his way to the bathroom. Having washed his hands and face, he looked at himself in the mirror. His blue eyes were slightly bloodshot and his greying hair unkempt. But other than that, his lean face looked quite good for eight o'clock in the morning.

"Happy birthday, boy." he told himself. "Forty-five today and not looking a day over ... " Some wrinkles on his brow caught his attention, then he stepped back to look at his not unsubstantial girth. " ... forty-five." He shrugged his shoulders and headed for the door, saying, "Ah well! Nobody's perfect." Then he turned to face himself in the mirror again and added, "But some of us come very close."

He dressed quickly and rushed downstairs. How many cards would there be this year? He had heard the postman talking to Mrs Johnson next door, so the cards should be waiting for him.

They should have been. Indeed, they would have been if Pat hadn't been to the front door, picked them all up and put them out of sight in her shopping bag, which now rested against the wall outside the back door.

Clive looked everywhere in the hallway for the cards before going into the kitchen to see if Pat had them. "Any post this morning?" he asked, without specifying what particular mail he was expecting. Well, there was no need to. Pat knew it was his birthday, didn't she?

"No," said Pat. "Why? Were you expecting anything?"

He shrugged his shoulders, expecting Pat to bring this tease to an end now. But all she did was turn back to the cooking.

Clive simply couldn't believe it. She knew it was his birthday. It came on the same date every year. Surely she couldn't forget. He never forgot hers. Well, only twice. And what about his brothers and friends? Had they forgotten too? No, they couldn't all forget, surely. Could they?

Clive was like a child who had lost his favourite toy. He was searching everywhere–drawers, cupboards, anywhere the cards could have been hidden.

"What are you looking for?" Pat asked him.

"Nothing," he replied, but continued his search.

Pat could feel a smile coming, so she turned back to the bacon in the frying pan. She had to keep a straight face. The others were depending on her. "How many eggs do you want?" she asked.

"Only one," said Clive. "I'd better take more care of myself now I'm getting older."

Pat nearly burst out laughing, but managed to restrain herself. "What's the matter, love? Aren't you feeling well?"

"Just feeling the years catching up on me," he said.

"We all feel that," Pat said and turned the bacon over.

Clive frowned as he watched her do this. Why didn't she take the hint? She must have forgotten completely. No, she wouldn't forget. Her card must be around here somewhere, even if there weren't any others.

The frown disappeared and Clive went to look behind a tray which was on the table and leaning against the wall. The tray slipped and knocked a plate to the floor. The plate smashed.

Pat jumped. She turned round to see what had happened. "Now look what you've done. That was one of the plates my mother gave us for Christmas."

"Good. That means only five more to go." Clive wasn't feeling particularly diplomatic now.

"What did you say?" Pat asked, moving on to the offensive.

"I said . . ."

"I know what you said. You probably did it deliberately. You've never liked those plates. You've never liked my mother. If she knew, she'd be very hurt."

Clive sniggered. "If she knew, I'd be very hurt. She'd put a spell on me."

"You'd better stop this, Clive, or you'll be sorry."

"There you are. Even you think she'll put a spell on me."

The bacon was sizzling in the frying pan, but nowhere near as much as Pat seemed to be now. "That does it," she said. "Enough is enough." She took off her apron and threw it at her husband. "Make your own breakfast. I'm going out." She moved towards the back door, then turned back and went to the fridge. She took out an egg. "And here's the egg you wanted," she said, throwing it at Clive.

He tried to catch it but failed and it smashed on the floor.

"And you call yourself a cricketer," scoffed Pat as she again made for the back door.

This time she did leave, picking up the shopping bag after she had closed the door. Her husband didn't move. He was still in shock.

Pat went immediately to see Jessica—in keeping with the arrangements they had made previously. She went to the Bevans' back door, tapped on it and went straight in. She always did that on her frequent visits there. It was almost like a second home to her.

Pat and Jessica were the best of friends in spite of the fact that there was a twenty-year age difference between them. They were the only two women who went to every home game at the cricket club and a close bond had developed from that. They often went out together as they shared a number of common interests in addition to the cricket, including the theatre, the cinema and clothes. Not a sale passed at any clothes shop within a twenty-mile radius of Marwen without a visit from "the terrible twosome".

People said that they couldn't have been closer had they been related. The two often joked about this. Pat would say they were like mother and daughter, but Jessica would immediately refute this, saying they were more like sisters.

Jessica was finishing washing the breakfast dishes when Pat came in. "Hi!" she said, obviously surprised. "I wasn't really expecting you to get away this quickly. How did you manage it?"

Pat went to sit on a nearby stool. "No problem. Once we start talking about my mother, there's a good chance we'll soon be arguing. That's what we did and here I am."

Jessica hardly stopped laughing as she heard what happened, especially the part about the egg. "Poor Clive!" she said. "Perhaps you should go back to see him. I mean, it is his birthday after all."

Pat shook her head. "No, let him feel sorry for himself for a while. We've got work to do."

Jessica fetched her coat and the two left to make their way down to the cricket club. On the way out Pat laughed.

"What's the matter?" Jessica asked her.

"I was just thinking about Clive. He's probably still trying to work out how to make his breakfast."

* * *

She wasn't far wrong. Making his own breakfast was not something Clive was used to doing. This was evident as he stood in front of the frying pan, holding an egg in one hand and a knife in the other, wondering what to do next. The bacon was still sizzling.

Clive looked at the egg, then at the knife. He must crack the shell of the egg. He knew that much. He wasn't stupid. But how hard should he hit the egg with the knife? He thought for a moment. A light tap should do it. He tried a light tap, but it didn't do it. The shell remained intact.

Try again. He did. Same result.

Obviously not hitting it hard enough. Right. here goes. Clive brought more force to bear this time. Too much force. The shell crumpled under the impact and Clive was left with egg all over his hand.

You win some, you lose some. Clive threw away what was left of the egg, then cleaned the mess on his hand. If at first you don't succeed, have another crack. Clive took another egg from the fridge. But as he was reaching for the knife, the egg slipped from his hand and fell to the floor. Another egg bites the dust!

Another mess. Another clearing exercise. Another egg? No way. Clive decided to have a bacon sandwich instead. He went to the bread bin, but his luck was still out. No bread!

Rather than give vent to his feelings, Clive took a deep breath. He was nothing if not adaptable. He would quite simply have a slice of bacon and a cup of tea. Nothing could go wrong with that.

He fetched the kettle, but before filling it, he put it back down. Why should he make do with something so simple? This was his birthday. He should have something special. Ideally, he should be celebrating his big day with the help of his wife and friends. But they had all forgotten, hadn't they? So why should he lose out? No, he would celebrate it on his own—and in his own way. A special breakfast was called for. Not bacon and tea for him. He was going to have bacon and gin. Now that would be special.

Clive fetched a quarter-full bottle of gin from a nearby cupboard and then went back to the frying pan. He lifted the bacon on to a plate and took both plate and bottle to the table. At last he could have his breakfast.

He picked up the bacon with his hand. He wouldn't have done that if he had thought about it. After all, the bacon had been in the frying pan for over quarter of an hour and so was quite hot. So hot that Clive let go of it.

Just like a child, he immediately put his burnt fingers in his mouth. Pity he couldn't have put his foot in his mouth as well. That would have prevented him from treading on his breakfast, which was now on the floor.

Clive kicked the meat away. "That does it. No bacon. I'll have gin and gin instead." He picked up the gin bottle and headed for the lounge. This breakfast business was very tiring.

* * *

Pat and Jessica worked hard at the club all morning. The big birthday cake had been delivered and various people had been down with sausage rolls, sandwiches, cakes, etc. By mid-day everything had been put into the committee room and would stay there until after the match had ended. Clive was not to know anything about a party until then.

"Are you going home now?" Jessica asked.

Pat shook her head. "No, I'll keep out of Clive's way until after the game."

"What about his lunch?"

"That," said Pat "is his problem."

* * *

Actually it was no problem at all for Clive. He was still drinking his breakfast. He had finished the original bottle and, having started another, was now singing "Happy Birthday" to himself.

* * *

When a home game had a two o' clock start, Marwen Cricket Club expected all its players to be at the club by half past one. It was now 1.33 pm and all the players were there except one. The captain was missing. This was unusual because more often than not Clive was the first to arrive.

The others thought that as it was his birthday, he may have been delayed by some celebratory lunch. Little did they know!

He would have to turn up soon, because he would need time to change. Unless he came down already changed. Yes, that could explain why he was a little late.

They were right about the changing. Clive had already changed into his kit and was now standing in front of a mirror, holding his bat and playing some imaginary strokes. He looked in good form.

Then an idea came to him. Why not get some real practice in before going down to the game? He went to the kitchen, placed a stool against a wall and put his bat to lean against the stool. The stool could be the wickets. But what about the ball? That was easy. Clive fetched an egg from the fridge.

He could now try his inswinger. He took a short run-up, then bowled the egg. It missed the bat and the stool and smashed against the wall. Not a very good inswinger!

"No ball!" shouted Clive.

Good. He had another chance now. He fetched another egg and tried again. This time the egg hit the bat. The bowling was getting more accurate.

Clive went back to the fridge. Only one egg left. Time for some batting practice. He fetched his bat and stood in the middle of the room. Bat in one hand, egg in the other. He threw the egg up in the air and on its way down hit it with an excellent hook-shot.

"A towering six by Clive Walters," he yelled, then acknowledged the cheers of the imaginary crowd.

There were no more eggs left, so he decided to make his way down to the ground.

* * *

In the meantime all the other players had changed and Temway's captain, David Davies, had twice been into the home team's changing room to see if Clive had arrived, so that the toss could take place to determine which team would bat first.

The minutes ticked away and the Marwen players started thinking that perhaps their skipper wasn't coming at all. Their fears were dispelled when Kevin Williams rushed in to say that Clive was on his way. Other fears immediately took their place, however when Kevin described the manner in which Clive was on his way.

The Marwen captain was swaying left, then right, then left again, at times trying to go both ways at the same time. And whichever way he was swaying, he was waving his bat above his head and shouting, "Here comes the King!"

Bob Evans and Arthur hurried outside and ran to take hold of their skipper. They guided him towards the changing room and managed to get him inside before anyone else saw what was happening.

Clive was put to sit on a chair. "What on earth have you been doing?" Arthur asked him.

"Having breakfast," Clive answered simply with a smile on his face.

Arthur looked at him in disbelief. "Breakfast?"

Clive nodded. "Bacon and gin—without the bacon."

Kevin said that he'd go and find a replacement for the obviously-indisposed captain. But Clive stopped him. "I'm playing," he announced.

"You can't," Arthur told him. "Not in that state."

"Yes, I can," insisted the captain and started to wave his bat again. "I've been practising today and I'm in pretty good form."

Kevin took the bat from him and looked at it in amazement.

A Good Catch

He couldn't understand what the yellow marks were.

In spite of further pleas from Arthur, Clive insisted that he was the captain and was going to play. He then got up, saying that he was going to see Temway's captain. He managed only two steps before falling to the floor.

Arthur picked him up and kept a tight grip on him. "Listen, Clive. If you insist on playing, you've got to put on a damned good act. Do you hear? If any of the others on the committee find out you're drunk–especially T.G.–you can forget about playing for Marwen again, let alone being captain."

"I'll be alright," Clive said firmly and pushed Arthur away. He managed two more steps before renewing his acquaintance with the floor.

Again Arthur picked him up. "I'm coming with you," he said. "And remember this–if you win the toss, we're batting. It'll give you more time to sober up."

Arthur turned to Kevin. "Get some coffee, Kev. Black. And plenty of it." Then he turned his attentions back to the captain. He kept a firm hold on him and guided him through the door.

* * *

The two captains and Arthur walked slowly to the wicket. David Davies thought it strange that Arthur was there but made no comment. He also thought there was something odd about Clive but couldn't put his finger on it.

Fortunately, the Temway captain liked the sound of his own voice, so Clive could keep quiet most of the time and just concentrate on where to put his five feet. He had never realised before that he had five. Walking could be such a complicated business at times.

The coin was tossed and David Davies called wrongly. Clive said that Marwen would bat first.

* * *

No sooner had Clive been put on the chair in the changing room than he was having black coffee forced on him by Kevin.

Arthur was talking to the opening batsmen, telling them to stay at the wicket for as long as possible in order both to build a solid foundation for the innings and to give the skipper time to sober up. As the batsmen left, the others in the room wished them luck. Clive got up, saying he was going out to watch them.

Arthur pushed him back forcefully. "You stay there and drink that coffee."

"Can I have some gin in it?"

This time Arthur yelled at him "Drink the coffee."

It was going to be a difficult task getting Clive through the afternoon without anyone finding out about his condition. It was to be made none the easier by the fact that T.G. wanted to have a word with the Marwen skipper. When Arthur heard T.G. approaching, he rushed outside to head him off. "Is Clive in there?" T.G. asked him.

"No," said Arthur without hesitation. "I don't know where he is. He's around the place somewhere."

When Clive heard this, he stood up and was about to tell them where he was. Kevin quickly got hold of him and put his hand over the skipper's mouth.

The door opened and Arthur came in. "Pour that coffee down him, Kev," he said. "Or we're all in trouble."

* * *

Each of the Marwen batsmen did his best to stay at the crease for a long time. Some succeeded, others failed. By ten past four the score had reached 94 for 6.

When the sixth wicket fell, Clive got up, ready to enter the fray. Usually it was he who went in when the sixth wicket fell and he fully intended doing so again today, even though he didn't have any pads on. Arthur, already wearing pads, pushed Clive back into the chair and picked up his bat. "More coffee, Kev," Arthur said and then walked out.

* * *

The innings continued and the allotted fifty overs were being used up well. The score had moved on to 138 for 8 when the last over of the innings began. If the two batsmen in the middle could survive this over, there would be no need for Clive to bat. Arthur was the non-striking batsman, Andy Jones was at the other end.

The first two deliveries of the over went harmlessly past the bat. The third one also went past the bat but hit the off-stump. Bowled! Clive would have to bat now. Arthur closed his eyes, dreading what would happen when the new batsman emerged from the changing room.

Clive managed to walk to the wicket without any assistance. Unfortunately, however, he went to the wrong end and came to stand alongside Arthur. Arthur pointed out the error to his captain, who then went to the other end, put his bat somewhere in front of the stumps and leaned on it. He didn't bother to take guard.

Clive was still leaning on the bat as the bowler ran up–and remained in that position as the ball flew past on its way to the wicket-keeper. There was still no movement from Clive as the next ball also went through to the wicket-keeper. But when the bowler delivered the final ball of the over–and the innings–tiredness got the better of Clive. The Marwen captain fell forward and as he did so, the bat moved with him. The ball struck the edge of the bat and sped to the boundary for four runs. The innings was over.

Standing alongside Kevin in the doorway to the clubhouse, T.G. wondered aloud why Clive hadn't gone in earlier so that he could have hit a few more shots like that. Kevin shrugged his shoulders.

T.G. started to move towards the players leaving the field to ask the captain himself, but Kevin grabbed him. "No, T.G. Come in here. I'll get you a pint." He knew full well that the chairman's inability to refuse a drink would outweigh any curiosity regarding the captain's tactics.

* * *

Arthur didn't bother to take off his pads as he would be needing them when he kept wicket after tea. He fetched some money from his jacket to pay for the tea and was getting ready to leave the changing room with Clive when he realised that his erstwhile batting partner wasn't ready to leave at all. The captain was lying on the table in the middle of the room sound asleep.

Arthur woke him up and pulled him to his feet. "Don't be anti-social now, Clive. It's time for your tea."

Clive was too tired to reply. Indeed, he was too tired to do anything. Arthur had to take off the skipper's pads and then guide him towards the clubhouse.

Clive sat between Arthur and Bob for the duration of the tea. Every so often he would tilt one way or the other. Then Arthur or Bob would dig him in the ribs to wake him up again. They managed to get him to eat a sandwich and a small cake. That and a cup of tea would have to keep him going during the post-tea session on the field.

Arthur didn't get to drink his own cup of tea. As he was lifting the cup, he saw T.G. moving towards them, so he and Bob got hold of Clive and quickly led him out through the back door.

* * *

With regard to the fielding, Arthur had worked out that the best way of dealing with the situation was to have Clive at first slip, with Kevin at second slip. So between them Arthur and Kevin could keep the tired captain on his feet and Arthur could give instructions to the other fielders as if he was passing on what Clive had told him.

As things turned out, Clive came into the picture only three times during Temway's innings. The first occasion was the very first ball of the innings, bowled by Andy Jones. Not that Clive knew much about it. The ball caught the edge of the bat and flew straight towards him in the slips. He, of course, was too tired to do anything about it. In fact, he didn't even see the ball coming. He did feel it though, when it hit him on the shoulder and knocked him back. Fortunately, the ball went into the air and Kevin caught it at second slip.

A Good Catch

The rest of the team ran over to congratulate the two slip-fielders, one of whom sat on the ground, wondering what all the fuss was about.

Temway had moved on to 73 for 5 when Clive next became a part of the play. John Price was bowling and Clive was fielding at leg-slip, still very tired. So tired that he fell asleep and sank to the ground. This at the very moment that the batsman hit the ball down the leg side. Clive, in his sleep, fell on the ball and stopped a certain boundary. The applause of the others woke him. They were all impressed. And amazed. Clive wasn't usually this good in the field.

The third incident occurred at the end of the innings, with the score at 103 for 9 and Marwen within sight of victory. They again had two slips—Clive and Kevin. As with the first ball of the innings, Andy managed to get the ball to move away, clipping the edge of the bat as it did so. The ball went straight to Clive, but he was half-awake by now and saw a red blur moving towards him. Although he fell backwards, he held on to the ball and Marwen had gained their first win of the season.

* * *

After showering and changing, the players made their way to the clubhouse. The last three to enter were Arthur, Kevin and Clive. This was no accident, as Arthur and Kevin had earlier been told by Pat to ensure that Clive went in last.

The skipper, less sleepy now after a refreshing shower, was taken aback by what he saw when he entered the clubhouse. It seemed as if all the members of the club were there and their wives, also the Temway team and quite a few villagers who didn't usually go to the cricket club. As he came in, they all sang "Happy Birthday". Then they moved to let Clive see the large birthday cake on the table in the centre of the room. So they hadn't forgotten after all!

Pat came to him and kissed him. "Happy Birthday, love," she said.

"Why didn't you say anything about this?" he whispered.

"It was meant to be a surprise." She kissed him again. "Sorry about the row this morning. I had to get down here without letting you know where I was going." She smiled. "And sorry about the egg."

Clive couldn't get any words out. All he could say was, "Mm."

Pat asked, "Did you manage your breakfast alright?"

"Mm."

"I hope there wasn't too much of a mess."

"Oh, no," Clive said quickly, then fell silent again. A picture came to his mind. A picture of a man bowling an egg at the wall in his kitchen.

T.G. now joined them and gave them a glass of champagne each. "Happy birthday, Clive," he said. "I've been trying to have a word with you all day. Anyway, never mind about that now. That was a good win out there. Well done, my boy."

Obviously all the disputes of previous weeks were now forgotten. T.G. turned to the rest of the people in the room and called for quietness. When all the chattering had died down, he spoke.

"I know you wouldn't want me to let this occasion go by without saying a few words." He ignored the groans which followed that statement and went on. "Well, Clive, this is a big day for you. The team has won its first game of the season, you had a good game yourself and to top it all, it's your birthday. So you've got plenty of cause to celebrate. And we're all here to make sure that you celebrate in style.

"There's no need for me to tell you how highly you're thought of here at the club. And, I may add, that includes yours truly, in spite of any disagreements we may have had lately." Everyone cheered. "Your attitude today has shown yet again how highly you regard this great club. Many people in your position would have said they were unavailable to play so that they could go off to enjoy themselves somewhere else. But not you, Clive. You're an outstanding example to us all."

Arthur and Kevin looked at one another.

T.G. continued. "I would therefore ask everyone to raise their glasses and salute a true gentleman. Happy birthday, skipper."

Glasses were raised and a shout of "Happy birthday, skipper" resounded around the room. This was followed by shouts of "Speech! Speech!"

T.G. pulled Clive forward. "Yes, come on, Clive. Let's have a few words."

Clive disliked speaking in public, but he couldn't get out of saying something now. "Well," he said, "I don't really know what to say . . . Thank you all for this surprise. And I can assure you that it was a surprise. My dear wife here said nothing. I was sure she'd forgotten." Everyone laughed. "Of course, I should've known better."

He put his hand to his chin and narrowed his eyes. "I suppose I should be worried that Pat can keep a secret so well. What else is she keeping from me?" Again the others laughed, especially after Pat hit her husband across the head with the palm of her hand.

When the laughter subsided, Clive continued. "You've all been very kind and I'm really grateful. As T.G. said, I could've gone elsewhere today. But I'm glad I didn't. I could've started celebrating hours ago. But I'm glad I didn't."

Arthur dropped his glass. People turned to see what had happened, then turned back to Clive. Arthur too looked at Clive and the captain was looking directly at him and smiling. Arthur was struck by the irony of the situation. The others would now be thinking that he had had a drink or two already, yet were convinced that Clive hadn't touched a drop all day.

The skipper went on with his speech. "I'm glad I played today. And I'm thankful that I've got such good friends." Again he was looking directly at Arthur. "It's good to have you here to help me celebrate. Thank you all."

Everyone applauded. Then they moved either towards Clive or towards the food. Arthur did neither. He went to fetch a cloth to clear up the mess on the floor.

* * *

As Clive was reading his cards, David Davies came to him. "Here you are, Clive," he said and handed him a glass. "One large gin and tonic for the birthday boy."

"Thanks, Dai," said Clive, picturing in his mind the gin bottles on the lounge table at home.

Clive took a sip of the drink. That did it. He headed straight for the toilet, where he promptly brought up what little food he had eaten at tea-time.

* * *

By nine o'clock the party was in full swing. Clive and Pat were sitting at a table with a few of the other players and their wives. On the table in front of Clive were three glasses of vodka and lime. People had wanted to buy Clive gin and tonic, knowing this to be his favourite drink, but he had told them that he'd prefer vodka and lime tonight. He knew he couldn't touch another drop of gin. Mind you, he hadn't as yet touched any of the vodka either.

Clive turned to Pat. "Listen, there's something I've got to talk to you about."

He didn't get a chance to say any more. T.G. had come over from the bar with another vodka and lime for him "Here you are, my boy. Compliments of the committee." T.G. put the glass alongside the others. "Doc paid, of course," he added.

Clive smiled. "Of course." He raised his hand to Doc, who was serving behind the bar.

The chairman returned to the bar and Clive returned to the business of trying to prevent the outbreak of another world war when he got home. "We've got to talk, Pat. It's important."

"Not now," his wife told him. "Relax, enjoy yourself. It's your party."

"But..."

"No, Clive. It can wait till we get home." Pat then turned to talk to one of the other women on the table.

Clive closed his eyes and pictured the mess in the kitchen. When he opened his eyes, he saw the four glasses of vodka in front of him "Ah well," he sighed and drank the lot, one after another. If World War III did break out later on, he, at least, was going to be completely oblivious to it.

Chapter 3

ONE MAIDEN TOO MANY

With the first win of the season under their belt, the Marwen players could look forward to their next game, away to Choreton. By one o'clock on the Saturday, however, things didn't look so rosy. Only ten players had arrived at the club ready to go to Choreton. There was no sign of Pete Richards, one of the opening batsmen.

No-one yet knew that Pete was at the hospital, having witnessed the birth of his first child. The baby girl weighed in at 7lb.5oz. and Pete and his wife, Julie, were admiring their offspring's obviously-healthy larynx.

But this noise was nothing compared to that made by T.G. in the car park of the cricket club when Jessica arrived with the news that Julie Richards had been taken to the hospital and Pete had gone with her, so he would be unable to play today.

"Why did he have to go?" yelled T.G. "He's not having the baby."

"Oh, come on, Dad," said Jessica. "He wanted to be with his wife at the birth of their first child. I think it's sweet."

"Sweet? I don't call it 'sweet'. I call it 'damned inconsiderate'. Cricket players' wives shouldn't give birth on a Saturday."

"You'd better put that up on the notice board for future reference," Jessica said. "Anyway, there's no problem. I've got my kit in the car. I'll play."

"You will not," said her father emphatically. "We've got a reserve who can play."

"No, we haven't," interjected Kevin. "Gareth's gone to Cardiff for the day. He's cheesed off with being reserve every week."

"Cheesed off!" yelled T.G. "I'll give him 'cheesed off'. He won't even be reserve from now on. Look at the mess he's left us in. I knew we shouldn't have let the Seconds go on that tour." He was referring to the fact that the Second XI had left the previous day to play a couple of matches in Oxford over the weekend.

When Jessica again suggested that she play, T.G. turned on her. "Will you shut up? I'm trying to think."

"What's there to think about?" she asked. "You're one short and I'm willing and able to play. You know I can do it."

"I've said 'No' and I mean 'No'. We need eleven *men* in the team."

"This is the 1970s, Dad. Things have changed since your day, in case you hadn't noticed."

Kevin took up Jessica's cause, telling the chairman that they had nothing to lose. Better to have Jessica in the team than be one short. What's more, he pointed out, Jessica had shown herself to be a more-than-adequate cricketer when practising with the players in the nets. Clive backed up Kevin's argument, but T.G. was adamant.

In the meantime Jessica had gone to her car to fetch her kit bag. She returned to find the argument still in a position of stalemate. She would have to think of something fast. She might never get an opportunity as good as this again. She held up the bag. "O.K., I'm ready."

"I've told you to shut up," T.G. shouted. "I'm trying to think of a way round this problem. We'll have to leave in a couple of minutes, full team or not."

"If you weren't so pig-headed, there'd already be a way round the problem."

T.G. didn't hear his daughter. He had come up with a solution of his own. "Let's go," he said. "We'll have a full team after all. I'll play. We can pick up my kit on the way."

The others looked at him in amazement. T.G. hadn't played any cricket in over ten years.

Jessica was the first to speak. "You can't be serious."

"I've never been more serious, my girl."

"But you're not fit enough to play."

"Neither are half the other players in the team. I'll be alright. I'll field in the slips."

Jessica wasn't giving in easily. "And what about your toe?" T.G. had been troubled by an infected big toe on his right foot for the past few days. At times it was so painful that he had difficulty walking.

T.G. smiled. "Thank you for your concern, my dear. But don't you worry, I'll be fine."

The smile turned to a grimace when Jessica dropped her kit bag on her father's right foot. T.G. was in agony. "What the hell...?" He couldn't say any more.

"Sorry, Dad. The bag slipped."

It took T.G. a while to recover from the 'accident'. But one thing was certain–He wouldn't be able to play cricket today. He turned to face his daughter. "You think you've been clever, don't you? Alright, so I can't play. But I'm damned certain you won't play either. We'll play one short rather than have a woman in the team."

Jessica was furious. Why wouldn't he give in? He could be as stubborn as a mule at times. "Determination", he called it. Well, she could be just as determined. Without saying anything, she walked to her father's car and, having checked that he had left the keys in it, she got in, reversed it out of its parking space and manoeuvred it so that it was facing the clubhouse wall. She then revved up the engine.

Her father limped towards her as quickly as he could. "What are you doing now?" he yelled.

"Nothing much. I'm just going to use that wall to reshape the front of your car. Unless you reshape your ideas about letting me play."

"You wouldn't dare." T.G. uttered the words, but he didn't

really believe them. He knew full well that his daughter would dare. She could do very strange things when she was in a temper. Anyone who knew her would vouch for that.

"Just you watch," she said as she revved up the engine again, moving her hand towards the hand brake.

"Alright! Alright!" shouted her father. "You win. You can play."

Jessica switched off the engine and got out of the car. "Thank you, Father," she said and went to pick up her bag.

* * *

A few minutes later three cars pulled out of the club car park. Clive and Kevin were taking their cars and Jessica was driving her father's. It was pointless taking a fourth car, so she left her own at the club.

On the way to Choreton Jessica drove behind Kevin. She was pleased he had spoken up for her earlier. Perhaps that this was an indication that at last he was beginning to take an interest in her. She had waited a long time for such a sign. She was quite sure that Kevin was the right man for her, even though the two of them had never been out together, other than as part of a crowd from the cricket club. Surely it was only a matter of time before he asked her out. Perhaps he still thought of her as T.G.'s little girl. But couldn't he see that T.G.'s little girl was now a young woman?

As she drove, Jessica thought of her two main ambitions in life: playing for Marwen's cricket team and marrying Kevin. She would achieve the first of those this afternoon. She hoped it wouldn't be too long before she achieved the other as well. She could see the wedding in her mind's eye. A grand occasion in the village. The church would be packed for the service...

T.G. was also anticipating a church service in the near future. But it wasn't a wedding. It was a funeral. His funeral. And it would be taking place within the next few days if Jessica didn't ease off on the accelerator as they approached the roundabout ahead–and the juggernaut that was at present on the roundabout.

"Slow down!" yelled T.G.

Jessica snapped back to reality and, for the first time, noticed the roundabout and the juggernaut. She slammed on the breaks and avoided an accident—but only just. The two passengers in the back seat could open their eyes again. Their prayers had been answered.

Shortly after half past one the cars arrived at Choreton's ground, one of the most picturesque grounds in the League. A row of oak trees ran alongside the boundary at one end of the ground, the clubhouse was at the other end. A little stream ran behind the trees, then rounded to the left before turning away towards a nearby river. The oak trees provided a welcome shade on hot summer days. Today was one such day, so there would be no shortage of volunteers to field on that part of the boundary.

The players moved towards the changing rooms and it was now that the first problem regarding Jessica's playing was mentioned. T.G. asked his daughter, "Where are you going to change?"

"With us, of course" John Price said immediately.

"That's right," added Arthur. "There's supposed to be equality nowadays."

"Thank you for the offer, gentlemen," Jessica responded, placing special emphasis on the word 'gentlemen'. "But I think I'll decline it for now."

"Why's that?" asked John.

"I can think of a couple of reasons," said Arthur.

Jessica decided it was time to leave this conversation and moved away towards the ladies' toilet. A couple of the Choreton players saw her go there with her bag but thought nothing of it. They were used to seeing Jessica coming with the Marwen team. It didn't cross their minds that today she'd be in the Marwen team.

Ten minutes later Jessica emerged, dressed proudly in her cricket kit, and went to join the rest of the team. Although quite short in stature, she was now walking tall. Her face was beaming and this served to add even more to her already attractive appearance. Her wavy brown hair, hanging at shoulder length, shone in the sunlight and with her slim figure, she looked very becoming in her all-white outfit. Little wonder that heads turned as she made her way over to the others.

It was now that the Choreton players realised that Jessica would actually be playing against them. And that's when the comments started. "You lot really are in a bad way this year. Even a woman can get into the team." "New tactic, eh? Trying to put us off our game." "At least she'll improve the team photograph."

The comments kept coming as more and more people realised what was happening. But the Choreton players made quite sure that Jessica was nowhere near when they made the comments. They had seen evidence of her temper on previous occasions.

Jessica wasn't the least bit concerned about what the opposition thought or said. Her mind was on the game. She couldn't wait for it to start.

Clive won the toss and elected to bat. The batting order was revised a little to cater for the fact that one of Marwen's usual openers wasn't playing. Bob Evans was to open instead of going in at No.3. Most of the other changes involved players moving one step up the batting order. Jessica was disappointed to find that she was going in at No.11. She knew that she could bat better than some of the others. But at least No.11 was better than not batting at all.

At 2.30 p.m. the game started, with Bob Evans facing Choreton's fastest bowler, McKenzie. After playing and missing the first ball, Bob comfortably lasted the remainder of the over, scoring two runs off the last ball. He now felt much better, having allayed his fear of being out for a duck in the first over.

In League matches there were fifty overs in each innings (if the batting team lasted that long), though at 5.10 p.m. the first innings was closed irrespective of the number of overs bowled. (However, a team which had not managed to complete fifty overs in that time would be reported to the League and be liable to a fine.)

Twelve points were awarded for a win and there were also bonus points available to both sides for batting and bowling. Every 40 runs scored secured a batting bonus point, while every two wickets claimed resulted in a bonus point for the bowling side.

Marwen hadn't gained many batting points this season,

A Good Catch

but today the batsmen were determined to bring about an improvement. Bob scored a fine 31 before being caught on the boundary and he was well supported by Ian Cowling and Carl Bevan (no relation to T.G.), both of whom reached 20. At 72 for 2 after 25 overs, Marwen looked set to build up their best score of the season. One batting point had already been secured and there was every chance of picking up at least another two.

However, once Cowling was bowled in the 26th over, the confidence seemed to drain from the team and the next 15 overs saw a dramatic collapse. By the end of the the 40th over Marwen had slumped to 78 for 8. They still had only one point.

Kevin Williams and Andy Jones were batting. Kevin was determined not to get out. He had been ever since reaching the crease and hearing one of the slip-fielders ask the wicket-keeper, "Is this the woman you said was playing for them?" When Kevin had played at the first delivery and missed it, the same fielder commented, "Yes, this is the woman alright."

Kevin kept calm in spite of the provocation. He was known to have a short fuse, but he was determined to keep his cool today—though in his mind's eye he'd planted his bat far enough down the slip-fielder's throat so that only the handle was showing.

With 10 overs to go, Kevin was 3 not out, Andy 1 not out and 2 runs still needed for the second batting point. It was up to them because there was only Jessica left to come in. Soon it was a matter of being up to Kevin and Jessica because Andy was caught behind off the first ball of the 41st over.

Choreton would now move in for the kill. Almost 10 overs to get the remaining wicket—and that one was a woman.

Jessica made her way to the wicket. Clive had told her not to worry. "Just go out there and enjoy yourself," he had said. "If we get the extra point, all well and good; if we don't, it's not your fault. There are plenty of others who deserve the blame, including myself. Good luck, Jess."

T.G. was nowhere to be seen as Jessica walked to the wicket. He was in the bar, making a start on drowning his sorrows.

Jessica ignored the wolf-whistles as she headed for the wicket.

When she reached the crease, the slip-fielder who had previously baited Kevin said, "So now there are two women batting."

Jessica looked directly at the fielder and said, "I suppose it's a pleasant change for you not to be the only one out here."

The fielder blushed as his team-mates laughed. He kept quiet after that.

Jessica wasn't put off by the field placings. In addition to three slips and a gully, there were two other close fielders in front of the bat on the off side and another two close in on the leg side. The only two fielders away from the bat were the bowler and the mid-on. Jessica wasn't bothered. She knew how hard she could hit the ball. A couple of good shots on her part would soon disperse the fielders.

The Choreton captain was the mid-on fielder and he warned the bowler, McKenzie, not to bowl any slower at Jessica. "If she's stupid enough to come out here, she can face the consequences. I'm warning you. Don't hold back."

He didn't. Neither did Jessica. She drove the ball between the two close fielders in front of her on the off side and the ball sped to the boundary. The second batting point had at last been gained. The Marwen players in and around the changing rooms cheered loudly.

Jessica drove the next ball equally hard, but this time there were no runs. It would have been another boundary if it hadn't hit the silly mid-off full on the left leg. The fielder dropped like a brick. He wished someone would go to the boundary to fetch his left leg back. But the excruciating pain that he was now feeling told him the leg was back already.

"Well fielded, Jim," shouted the captain as he moved from mid-on to survey the damage.

"Oh, bugger off, Andy," Jim replied.

It was obvious to one and all that Jim wouldn't be able to carry on after such a blow. More obvious to Jim than to anyone. He tried to stand up with the help of one of the others, but it was hopeless. He would have to be carried off–and would probably need an X-ray to check whether anything was broken.

A Good Catch

Jessica offered some sympathetic words. She had known Jim for years. Jim managed a slight smile.

"Don't worry about it," the Choreton captain told her. "It wasn't your fault. It wasn't anyone's fault."

"It was your bloody fault," Jim hissed at his captain. "You should have moved us back after seeing she can bat."

Jim was carried off and play was resumed. The Choreton captain kept an attacking field. Jessica turned to the slip-fielder who had made a comment when she came in. Pointing to the spot where Jim had been fielding, she said, "Why don't you come and field here instead?" Again the others laughed, again the slip-fielder blushed.

McKenzie had seen that Jessica liked to drive, so he pitched the next ball a lot shorter. Not a very sporting thing to do. He regretted it almost immediately. Not because it was unsporting, but because Jessica obviously could hook as well as she could drive. The ball was on its way to the boundary again. After that even the Choreton captain began to take Jessica's batting more seriously and readjusted his field placings.

It was now that a flaw in the batswoman's batting became apparent. She tapped the next ball on the leg side and called for a run. Kevin yelled at her to go back, but she kept coming. He ran as quickly as he could. Fortunately, the fielder running in from mid-wicket mis-handled the ball and by the time the throw came in, Kevin had managed to reach the crease. He glared at his batting partner, but she didn't notice this.

When Kevin played the final ball of the over to the off side, Jessica started running again. "Get back!" he yelled at her. This time she did turn back—and reached safety just before the ball came in.

It was the end of the over and somehow they had survived. Kevin wasn't slow to come down the wicket to inform his partner that they didn't have to score off every ball. There were nine overs left and they should try to use up as many of them as possible.

As it turned out, they used them all up. After 50 overs the score had reached 121 for 9. Choreton had failed to get the extra bowling point, yet Marwen had managed to gain a third batting point.

Kevin (22 not out) and Jessica (18 not out) were warmly applauded off the field after their magnificent effort. Kevin stepped aside to let Jessica go off first.

* * *

Clive was the first to congratulate Marwen's latest batting recruit. She herself was too excited to say anything.

Kevin said, "Well, skip, you've seen what we can do. It looks as if you've got a new opening partnership for next week."

"Are you volunteering?" Clive asked.

"On second thoughts, no" Kevin replied. "With her policy of running everything, I don't think my legs could stand it. I'd either be carried off or run out."

Jessica had just taken off one of her pads and she now threw it at Kevin.

"You've got it wrong there, Kev," said the captain. "It's the opposition that's carried off when our Jess is around."

Kevin laughed, but Jessica asked, "How is Jim?"

"His leg'll be sore for a few days," Clive answered, "but he'll be alright. He won't be able to bat though."

Kevin said, "Good tactics, Jess. Cut 'em down when you're batting and you won't need to worry about 'em when you're bowling." At which point Jessica's other pad hit him on the side of the head.

* * *

The Marwen players were quite confident as they sat down for their tea. It was the batting which had let them down so far this season, the bowling wasn't too bad. So they felt that they had every chance of bowling Choreton out for less than 121.

Little did they know that in a short while a disease was going to manifest itself. which would stay with them for much of the season. The team was to become subject to an epidemic of dropped catches.

In the early stages of the Choreton innings everything seemed to be going well for Marwen. Both the Choreton opening batsmen were dismissed cheaply and after ten overs Choreton were struggling at 24 for 2.

It was then that the disease struck. Andy was bowling the eleventh over and with the third ball of the over he should have gained his second, and his team's third, wicket. The ball struck the outside edge of the bat and went straight to Kevin at first slip. It should have been a straightforward catch, but Kevin snatched at it and the ball went to ground.

It was unusual for Kevin to drop a catch. He normally had such a safe pair of hands. He tried to put the miss to the back of his mind, consoling himself with the reasoning that he would catch far more than he would drop during the season.

But he could find no way of consoling himself in the 15th over when he dropped another catch. Same batsman. Same stroke. Same result.

At that point Kevin asked to be moved from the slips. He changed places with Clive, who had been fielding at mid-on.

After another two overs Clive decided to vary the approach and brought on John Price to bowl off-spin. It seemed as if the change was to bring immediate reward. On the fourth ball of the over the batsman was tempted into a rash stroke. he hit the ball high and long—and Andy was waiting for it on the long-on boundary.

He kept his eye on the ball, positioned himself correctly and did everything right. Everything, that is, except catch the ball. He couldn't explain how he managed to drop it, but drop it he did.

The Choreton batsmen couldn't believe their luck and steadily added more and more runs, gradually putting their team in a good position to win the match. After 20 overs Choreton had reached 73 for 2.

Clive now decided to use spin at both ends and brought on Bob to replace Andy, who was tiring and getting some hefty punishment from the rejuvenated batsmen.

Bob's first delivery was much too short and the batsman pulled it hard and high to the mid-wicket boundary for what he hoped would be six runs. He hadn't hit it hard enough, however, and John Price, fielding on the mid-wicket boundary moved to his right to be in position to take the catch.

Clive was glad that it was the experienced spin bowler fielding out there. After what had gone on before, one of the younger players might have panicked and dropped the ball. John didn't panic–but he still dropped the ball. Also the ball crossed the boundary after he had dropped it, so four more runs were added to the score.

Clive just couldn't believe it. What was happening to the team? He called for greater concentration from his players.

There was a short delay while Bob adjusted his boot-laces and Clive took this opportunity to speak to Arthur about the dropped catches. "Perhaps there was something in the tea," Arthur quipped.

But Arthur had drunk the tea as well and in the next over the symptoms of the disease appeared in him. The batsman tried to cut John's rather short delivery. The ball caught the top edge of the bat and went through to the wicket-keeper, but somehow he managed to drop it.

Clive looked up to the skies. "Who next?" he muttered. The answer to that: Clive himself. He was fielding at mid-on in Bob's next over. The ball was hit straight at him, but he reacted too slowly and another chance was gone. The score moved steadily on to 96 for 2. Each of the Marwen players was hoping the ball would come nowhere near. Each one, that is, apart from Jessica. She was amazed at what she'd seen. She only hoped that she'd have the chance of a catch. She'd show them.

And she did. She was fielding at mid-off to John Price's bowling when the ball was driven hard towards her. It was a chance similar to that which Clive had put down earlier. But Jessica made no mistake. 96 for 3.

The bowler ran over to her and kissed her on the cheek. So surprised were the rest of the players that a catch had actually been taken that they all came over to congratulate the catcher.

Arthur chuckled. "No wonder we're all dropping catches today. We're scared stiff that if we take one, the bowler's going to come over and kiss us."

Clive rearranged the field a little for the new batsman, bringing some men closer. There was virtually no chance of winning the game, but another wicket would bring a second bowling point.

The score had progressed to 109 for 3 when Jessica took another catch, this time a more spectacular one. The ball didn't rise very much as it came towards her at mid-off, so she had to dive forward to catch it. But even though the catch was of a higher standard than her first one, this time John didn't kiss her. Why should he? It was off Bob's bowling.

Choreton now needed only 13 more runs to win. It took them another four overs to reach their target. Yet in those four overs two more catches went down. In the end Marwen lost by six wickets.

Marwen's players were glad to leave the field. They didn't want to see a cricket ball for some time again. They were sickened by their display and were very subdued as they showered and changed.

Marwen's "person of the match", however, was far from subdued. She was singing merrily as she changed in the ladies' toilet. 18 not out and two catches. That would show them!

In the Choreton clubhouse afterwards Jessica was the centre of attention. One after another, people came up to her to congratulate her on her performance. "Marwen should play more women in the team," the Choreton chairman told her. "They might win more matches then."

But it was the comments of the Marwen chairman which gave Jessica most satisfaction. T.G. had kept away while others had been milling around his daughter, then when he saw the chance to speak to her alone he came over. Remembering that she would be driving him home, he put a glass of pineapple juice in front of her and said, "Well done, young lady! You proved me wrong and I'm not afraid to admit it." He paused before adding, "I'm so proud of you."

With tears coming to his eyes, T.G. kissed his daughter. "You deserve all the praise you get. And I for one will make sure that the whole of Marwen knows what you did here today."

Jessica could say nothing. There were tears in her eyes too. She knew what it had taken for her father to admit he was wrong and to say what he had said. He was a very proud man and it took a lot of courage for him to admit his mistake.

(It had, in fact, taken twelve whiskies to give him the courage to admit his mistake.)

Chapter 4

ALL OUT!

At the following Monday's committee meeting there were various other issues to be discussed prior to the selection of the team for the next match, at home to Brynteg.

One of these issues was the possibility of securing the services of an overseas player for the club. This had been mentioned in casual conversation in the past but now it was decided to give the idea a full and formal airing at committee level.

Everyone on the committee felt that it would be a good idea. If a player of better ability was brought to the club, it could help to bring the best out of the existing members of the team. But there were two important questions to consider. How would they go about finding such a player? And how much would it cost the club? The latter question, of course, was of paramount importance.

Doc provided some information in relation to the first question. Apparently there was an agent somewhere in the north of England who acted as an intermediary between clubs seeking overseas players and players from other countries who wanted to come to play club cricket here. Doc didn't know the agent's name or where in the north of England he was to be found.

Glyn James suggested that he could contact the secretary of Temway Cricket Club about this as they had had a spin bowler from Pakistan in their team two years previously. He seemed to remember something being said at the time about an agent in the north, so he could make enquiries and report back to a future meeting.

No-one knew anything about the cost involved. Doc said that some players wanted to play here so badly that they were prepared to play for a lot less than the full fee. whatever that might be, provided that they could have somewhere to stay.

Clive now mentioned something he had intended bringing up previously but had forgotten. His brother, who had emigrated to Australia twenty years previously, had recently told him over the phone that there was a young Australian playing for their local cricket team who wanted to come to Britain to play. As he had always wanted to see Britain and wasn't short of money, he'd be prepared to play for a suitable club for next-to-nothing. Clive said that he'd contact his brother to find out more and the matter was set aside for now until further information could be gathered.

The next item on the agenda was what T.G. called "a revolt among the servants", The women who made the teas during home matches were threatening to withdraw their services.

They had been complaining for some time about the facilities in the kitchen, and in particular the boiler. At various times during the past couple of seasons things had gone wrong with the boiler, but each time it had been patched up instead of replaced. Time and again the women had asked for a new boiler, but on each occasion the committee had decided that money could not be made available and so the old boiler would be patched up again.

It was a joke at the club that they had a political boiler because it had had so many leaks, but following the latest leaks few were prepared to laugh, especially among the women. The incident had occurred the previous day while the women were preparing the tea for a youth match. The boiler had leaked and Pat Walters's hand had been slightly scalded. It could have been much worse and as far as the women were concerned this was the last straw. With Pat leading the way, they had told T.G. they would refuse to use that boiler any more. Either a new one was installed in time for the next match or there would be no tea at that match.

T.G. had suggested that if they were so adamant about not using the boiler, they could boil the kettle a number of times. It would take longer, but if that's what would make them happy...

The tone of their reply, not to mention the language used, showed T.G. that his flippancy was not appreciated. He promised them he would mention it to the committee. Pat told him he would need to do more than mention it because the message from the women was clear: "No boiler, no women to make the tea".

T.G. duly informed the rest of the committee who listened for the most part with a smile on their faces. They had been along this road many times previously: the women made antagonistic noises, the boiler was repaired and the women went back to making the tea.

Clive advised caution this time. "They're really determined," he said. "They won't be fobbed off any more. Either we get a new boiler or we'll have no tea on Saturday."

"Is that you talking or Pat?" Arthur asked.

Clive smiled. "Pat has been stating her case quite strongly since yesterday, I admit. But she's got a point. It could have been a nasty accident."

"But thankfully it wasn't," T.G. said, "and we have to make sure that such a thing doesn't happen again. The women deserve our support."

Clive started to consider which doctor could be called. T.G. was obviously in a very bad way. But the chairman hadn't finished. "We'll get the boiler seen to immediately and whatever needs doing to it will be done. In plenty of time for Saturday's game."

Clive responded immediately. "But surely we should now be thinking in terms of getting a new boiler. This one's had a really good innings."

"Ordinarily I'd agree," said T.G. calmly. "But if you bear in mind that the next item on the agenda concerns buying some new kit for the team, you can appreciate that this makes the position more awkward."

Doc, as treasurer, came in here. "T.G.'s right. We haven't got enough money to buy new kit and a boiler. It's got to be one or the other."

"How essential is getting new kit?" Glyn asked.

"We need two new bats at the very least," Clive answered. "Three would be preferable. And then there's..."

Before Clive could go on T.G. interrupted. "And that's something I don't understand. How on earth are the bats going so quickly? It's certainly not through coming into contact with the ball."

Clive ignored the comment. "We need at least one other set of pads. And the keeper's gloves are split, so they need replacing."

"I'll drink to that," said Arthur.

Doc outlined the club's current financial situation and then summed up the problem by saying, "If we spend money on all that kit, we certainly won't have enough left to get a new boiler."

"The women aren't going to take that as an excuse," said Clive.

"They'll have to," said the chairman. "Who's this club being run for—the team or the women? If there's a choice between a new boiler for the women and necessary kit for the team, we've got to come down on the side of the team." Looking directly at Clive, he added, "Don't you agree, Clive. You're the captain."

There was only one answer Clive could give. And he knew that in giving it he was setting himself up for a period of hell at home. The decision was unanimous. The new kit would be bought immediately and the old boiler would be repaired.

"What about the tea for Saturday?" Clive asked.

"The women will come round, don't worry," T.G. replied positively. "They always do."

"I wouldn't be so sure," said the captain. "Not this time."

"You have a word with Pat. Make her see sense."

"I've got a better idea, T.G. You come home with me afterwards, then *you* can make Pat see sense."

T.G. declined the invitation. The others smiled. Apart from Clive, that is. He knew what lay ahead of him.

The committee moved on to the selection of the team for the coming Saturday's match against Brynteg. It didn't take them long to decide on an unchanged team. In spite of the collapse of the middle order in the last game, there were signs that the batting was improving. Pete Richards was now available again, but in view of the way Jessica had played on Saturday they couldn't really leave her out. The decision was again unanimous. As T.G. said, "We've got to have one in the team who can catch."

* * *

That night Clive went home a worried man. After all, he knew Pat better than anyone. She was easy-going and easy to please, on the whole. She tried to be helpful and accommodating. On the whole. Her attitude was that there were always two sides to an argument and a person should respect the opposing viewpoint. On the whole.

But, and this was a very big but, if she ever set her mind to something which she was utterly convinced was right, then woe betide anyone who stood in her way. Clive could remember only three occasions previously when such a situation had arisen. Number Four was coming up. And Number Four was going to be much worse than any of the others because this time Clive was one of the people standing in Pat's way.

Having been given the news, Pat's reply was immediate and forceful. She left Clive in no doubt that he should have stood by her on this issue and accused him of thinking more of the team than of his wife. Having made her point verbally, she then made her point silently. She didn't utter another word until the next morning when she said "Good morning"–to the postman.

* * *

It was now Wednesday evening and the silence was still unbroken. Each time Clive would try to start a conversation, Pat would either walk away or continue doing whatever she was doing as if nothing had been said. Clive was still waiting for the thaw to come as they sat down for their evening meal.

"Could you pass the salt, love?" he asked.

Pat slammed the salt cellar on the table in front of her husband.

Clive didn't really need to shake the cellar over his food. Enough salt had rained down on it when Pat had slammed the cellar down.

Obviously the thaw was still a long way off. But Clive knew he'd have to talk to Pat about the problem soon, because if the women persisted in their refusal to make the tea on Saturday other arrangements would have to be made.

"I saw T.G. this afternoon," Clive said. "The boiler's been repaired. so it'll be alright for Saturday."

Pat looked directly at her husband and, emphasising each word, said "That is of no concern to me."

Clive refused to be intimidated. Or rather, he refused to show that he was intimidated. "It means there'll be no danger of you scalding yourself on Saturday."

Again the reply came in an emphatic tone. "I know there'll be no danger of that. Because I shall not be anywhere near the boiler on Saturday. Nor any other Saturday."

"Come on, Pat. This has gone on long enough. Give us a break. We'll get a new boiler as soon as we can. I promise. This time we had to give the kit priority."

"Then let the kit make the tea on Saturday."

"Don't talk so daft." The words were out before Clive could think. He knew he shouldn't have said it. And he knew it was now too late.

"Very well," Pat replied. And the silence returned.

* * *

Clive had agreed to meet T.G. at the club that evening to let him know what the situation was. Glyn and Arthur were there too. Doc couldn't make it; he wasn't feeling well.

Clive told the other three that alternative arrangements would be necessary for the tea during Saturday's match. Pat wouldn't give in. T.G. had spoken to some of the other women. Their attitude was at one with Pat's.

Glyn was as practical as ever. "In that case we'll have to make the teas ourselves. It should be OK. If a group of us can get down here earlier than usual on Saturday, we can make the sandwiches, cut the cakes and get most of the work done before the match starts. T.G. and I can see to the tea while the first innings is going on and everything'll be ready by the time the players leave the field.

"Quite" said T.G. smiling.

It sounded so easy. Too easy, Clive thought. And he was right.

* * *

When Clive told Pat that the men were going to make the teas, she said nothing. But that was in keeping with every other "conversation" they had had since Monday night.

Clive couldn't remember Pat keeping a feeling of animosity for so long. It was a strain on Pat too. Many a time she had wanted to smooth over their differences in this matter. But she knew she had to make a stand. If she gave in now, she could never hope to win. It was a matter of principle. The women had had to put up with second best for too long. Something had to be done. And now was the time to do it.

Hard as it was, she had to keep the pressure on until the men gave in. They probably wouldn't before Saturday. They'd try to make a go of it themselves. But then they'd find out how much the women actually did. Perhaps then they'd appreciate the women more. Perhaps then they'd think more seriously about a new boiler.

She had no doubt whatsoever that they'd make a mess of things on Saturday. The only one of them who could possibly have coped was Doc–and he was confined to bed for at least a week with a serious chest infection.

The other four couldn't hope to manage on their own. Who'd pick up the bread? Who'd fetch the tomatoes, lettuce, cucumber, ham, cakes? Who'd remember to fetch the tea? There was no tea left in the clubhouse. Did they remember that she had the only key to the cupboard in which the crockery and cutlery were kept? There had been another key but that had gone missing. T.G. was going to get a duplicate made but he kept forgetting. Pat had intended seeing to it herself, but in view of recent events, well why should she?

* * *

The problems Pat had foreseen did indeed create difficulties. But the four healthy committee members were not to know this when they met at the clubhouse at half past twelve on the Saturday.

"Where do we start?" asked T.G.

"Best to start with the sandwiches," Glyn advised. "Who's fetched the stuff?"

Clive closed his eyes and groaned. Why hadn't he thought of that? How could he, of all people, forget that Pat picked up the bread, cakes and contents of the sandwiches on her way to the ground on a Saturday?

He opened his eyes and looked at each of the others in turn, hoping against hope that one of them had had more foresight than he. No such luck. He was out through the door like a bullet. And the bullet was back through the same door with the goods within a quarter of an hour. They still had plenty of time.

As he unloaded the groceries, Clive suggested that it wouldn't have strained the others too much to have put the plates and cutlery ready.

"How could we?" T.G. replied. "You've got the only key to the cupboard."

"No, I haven't."

"Your wife has. Didn't you get the key from her?"

Clive closed his eyes again. This wasn't his day. "I didn't think to," he said. "Anyway, you said you were getting a duplicate made to keep behind the bar."

"I haven't got round to it yet," blustered the chairman. "I've had too many other things to do. More important things."

"Tell that to the players when they're looking for their tea later on," said Arthur.

The bullet went through the door again. But this time it took Clive over half an hour to return. Pat had gone to visit a friend, so it had taken some time to find her.

By half past one the new caterers had made a start on the

sandwiches. But Clive and Arthur then had to go to get changed, so T.G. and Glyn had to manage on their own for a while. Clive promised that if he won the toss Marwen would bat, so that there'd be more people available to help with the food. Win the toss he did and Marwen batted.

Jessica was pleased to see that she had been moved up the batting order and would go in at No. 8. Clive was due in at No. 7, so he and Jessica could help with the food for some time before they'd be needed on the field–hopefully.

Jessica had been unsure about helping in the kitchen, her loyalties being somewhat divided now that she was a member of the team. That's why she had made herself scarce until it was time to go to the ground ready for the game. When Clive told her she could now help with the food, she had nowhere to hide from her dilemma. But when Kevin offered his services in the kitchen, her dilemma was resolved. After all, his offer might have been made in order to be closer to her. Actually, it was made in order to be closer to the food. He hadn't eaten since nine o' clock.

Bob Evans and Ian Cowling opened the batting and they did well, putting on 40 runs before Ian fell l.b.w. for 13.

Progress was also being made in the kitchen. Glyn had never buttered so much bread in his life. He and Jessica were working on the sandwiches. So was Kevin, though he was eating them rather than making them. He did stop, however, when Glyn threatened him with the knife he was using to butter his sixtieth slice of bread.

Clive was sorting out the cakes. T.G. was sitting in the bar, drinking whisky. The others had banished him from the kitchen, as he had been getting on their nerves, telling them the best way to do this and the quickest way to do that. Before leaving he had filled the boiler, which seemed to be working alright.

Outside, the score had moved on to 57 for 2, Carl Bevan having been bowled for 10. Bob was looking comfortable on 26.

Kevin excused himself from the kitchen in order to go and put his pads on. He grabbed another sandwich as he left. By the time he returned the score was 70 for 3. Clive would have to go to get himself ready.

Before Clive had had a chance to leave, someone shouted from outside, "You're in, Kev. Bob's out." Clive told Kevin to take his time and stay at the crease for as long as he could. For one thing Marwen needed someone to steady the innings, for another Clive needed time to get his pads on.

It was the other batsman, Barry Roberts, Clive should have told to take his time, because within a couple of minutes Barry was on his way back to the changing room, having been caught behind the wicket slashing needlessly at a delivery wide of the off-stump. The score was 73 for 5. Another collapse was under way.

It was up to Clive to stop the slide and this he did. After a nervous start he began to play with more confidence than he had shown all season. His timing had returned and some of his strokes were a pleasure to watch. One in particular had everyone applauding, a cover drive which was stuck so smoothly that it was well on its way to the boundary before any of the fielders had moved.

Kevin was content to play second fiddle as he watched his skipper play the bowling with such ease. He'd never seen Clive play like this before. Perhaps they should get him to make the food at every home game!

Clive seemed set for a half century at least, but with his score on 21, and the team's on 106, he firmly drove the Brynteg off-spinner back down the wicket. The bowler dived low to his right to take an amazing catch. Brilliant, exclaimed the Brynteg players. Sod, muttered Kevin under his breath. Still Clive had served notice that his confidence and form were well and truly back.

The scene was now set for a repeat of last week's partnership between Kevin and Jessica. Kevin hoped she'd make a more patient start this time. And fair play to her, she did allow the first ball to go through to the wicket keeper. She noticed that the ball turned slightly off the pitch, but not enough to cause concern.

The next ball was dispatched to the boundary and the following delivery would have gone as well had it not been stopped by a fielder just short of the line.

A Good Catch

"Here we go again," thought Kevin. He had a word with her at the end of the over, suggesting that she cool down a little. She did her best to obey.

Then, with the score at 135 for 6, she played forward to the off-spinner and the ball just popped up to give the bowler an easy return catch. Jessica was annoyed. They weren't letting her play her normal game. She wanted to go for her strokes as often as possible, yet she was being told to restrain this inclination. What was the point? She had scored only 11 today, but she could have scored a lot more if she hadn't held back. She'd have to have a word with Clive about this.

In the meantime Clive himself was trying to cope with another problem that had arisen in the kitchen. The food had all been set out on the plates, but when Glyn had gone to make the tea, he discovered that there was no tea anywhere in the kitchen. He was in a panic, T.G. was yelling at the top of his voice, and it was left to Clive to bring some calm to bear on the situation. He told Glyn to go to the shop immediately.

"There's no time," replied the flustered secretary. "They'll be off before long."

Clive remained calm. "Just go and get the tea. Leave the rest to me."

Glyn left and Clive set about pouring umpteen glasses of orange squash. He told T.G. to fetch ice from the fridge and put some in each glass.

By the time Glyn's car returned through the gates, the players were leaving the field. Marwen were all out for 148 with Kevin again undefeated on 26.

The Brynteg players sat down for their meal and T.G. and Clive brought in the squash. A few of the players were perspiring freely after their stint in the field and were glad to see the iced squash. Others, however, were surprised at not having the choice of squash or tea.

"Haven't you got anything warmer, Clive?" asked John Lewis, the Brynteg captain.

"We've got squash without ice," Clive replied quickly.

Everyone laughed—except T.G. He was in a foul mood.

"I meant tea actually," the visiting skipper said. "I like tea with sandwiches."

Clive lanced in the direction of the kitchen and could see Glyn getting to work on the tea. "Tea it is, John. It'll be in now. Glyn's pouring it"

Lewis then made the mistake of commenting on the absence of the women. "Are they on strike or what?"

T.G. glared at him and slammed down the last glass of squash, spilling half its contents. He stormed off without saying a word. Clive sat down and explained to his Brynteg counterpart what had happened. As they were talking, T.G. returned. "How many want tea?" he growled.

John felt like making a comment but thought the better of it. Six players indicated their desire to have a cup of tea. T.G. growled again and left. The two captains renewed their conversation.

After tea most of the Marwen players left to practise their catching on the field. This was Kevin's idea. They needn't have bothered. During Brynteg's innings, six catches were dropped in the first hour alone, one of them by Kevin himself. Indeed, by now almost everyone had dropped a catch in either or both of the last two matches. The one exception was Jessica.

After 25 overs Brynteg had reached 98 for 3. The wickets had fallen as a result of one l.b.w. decision, one run-out and one catch, when Jessica had kept her record intact. John Price had taken one wicket, but could have had at least another four had catches not gone to ground.

In the 26th over there were even more problems for Marwen. Andy Jones had come back for his second spell and Clive was fielding close in on the leg side. The third ball of the over was a little short and the batsman hooked it. The ball hit Clive full in the face before rebounding up in the air. Everyone stopped as the Marwen skipper fell backwards, blood pouring from a gash above the eye.

As it turned out the ball went as far as gully, where Bob was fielding. But Bob couldn't care less where the ball was, He ran straight over to Clive, knowing this was no minor injury. For the first time in years the stretcher, which was kept in the kitchen, was to be used. Kevin and Andy ran to fetch it. It was obvious to everyone that this was to be a hospital job.

Bob knelt over his captain. Clive was very dazed but was trying to say something. Bob moved closer and could just make out the words. "Did... anybody... catch it?"

Bob could hardly believe his ears. "Of course nobody caught it. We were too concerned about you."

"Fools," whispered the captain. "Catch... ball... first... then..." He passed out before completing the sentence.

Glyn had phoned for an ambulance almost immediately and it was on its way before Clive had been stretchered from the field. One of the Brynteg players was a doctor and he did what he could while they awaited the arrival of the ambulance.

Clive regained consciousness on the way to hospital. The doctor in A&E examined him thoroughly and found no serious injury. Clive had been very lucky. The cut required six stitches but it was unlikely that any other treatment would be needed. They would, however, keep him in for twenty-four hours for observation. This was a necessary precaution owing to the fact that he had actually lost consciousness for a period. They wanted to be sure everything was alright before releasing him.

T.G. and Glyn had gone to tell Pat and then Glyn had driven the three of them straight to the hospital. There were tears in Pat's eyes as she went in to see her husband. "You damned fool," she told him.

He smiled. "Don't call me a damned fool. Call Bob a damned fool. He didn't take the catch."

"I don't care about any catch. All I care about is you." Pat held her husband's hand tightly and nothing more was said. Clive had just been given a sedative and before long he was sound asleep.

Pat went out to the corridor to tell T.G. that he and Glyn could go. Glyn was talking to a nurse further down the corridor. Pat said that she would stay with Clive until he woke up. T.G. offered to stay with her, but she told him he should go back to the club. "The others will want to know how things are. You can tell them face to face rather than over the phone. Tell them the fool is going to be alright."

T.G. held her hand for a moment, then moved away slowly. He had obviously been really shaken. He moved down the corridor towards Glyn.

"Oh, T.G.!" Pat called after him. The chairman turned and Pat went on. "You can stop worrying about the tea problem. If Clive is intent on killing himself, I want to be close at hand. I'll be there to make the tea from now on."

T.G. said nothing. He couldn't even manage a smile. He remained silent all the way back to Glyn's car, but while walking he determined that a way would be found to buy the kit *and* a new boiler.

Clive slept soundly for four hours, oblivious to the fact that Pat was sitting at his side throughout–and oblivious to the fact that Marwen had lost the match by five wickets. Two more catches had gone down and one had been taken–by Bob Evans.

Chapter 5

ALL'S FAIR IN LOVE AND CRICKET

The next match was the big one–Ramley at home. Each season the people of Marwen looked forward to this fixture as an opportunity to rub their local rivals' noses in it again, but this season they weren't looking forward to it so eagerly. Marwen Cricket Club's slump had raised serious doubts as to their ability to see off the team from Ramley. Still, this was a local derby and with local derbies the form book goes out the window and anything can happen.

In spite of the injury sustained in the Brynteg game, Clive was determined to play in the "big one". He had refused to take even one day off from work. He worked in the Human Resources Department in a local glassware factory and when he had gone in on the Monday morning they told him he should go home and stay there for a few days, in case there was any delayed reaction. Clive refused, he didn't want anyone having any doubts as to his fitness.

Pat knew how desperate he was to play, so she didn't try to dissuade him. The committee had met on the Monday evening and asked Clive to consider seriously the wisdom of playing so soon after the injury. But Clive was adamant. He was playing.

Throughout the week people in the village came up to him to wish him all the best for Saturday. "Don't let us down, boy, we're counting on you." "You show 'em Saturday." "Let 'em know what we're made of in Marwen."

It was a game the team dare not lose. To win meant holding the local bragging rights, at least until the return fixture. The people of Marwen could then grasp every opportunity to remind any friends in Ramley that Marwen was *the* place to live. To lose meant that heads would be hung in shame. It meant having to put up with incessant jibing from those friends in Ramley. It meant being told you were second best. No, to lose was unthinkable.

Local derbies produce intense rivalry in any sport. Football, rugby, hockey, cricket, dominoes. Whatever the game, the priorities are the same. Number one is making sure that you win, number two is making sure that if you can't win you don't lose.

Whenever people from the two villages met during the week, the conversation invariably turned to Saturday's contest. The players too lost no opportunity to have digs at their opponents. Clive had taken Pat to Swansea for a meal on the Wednesday evening and as they were leaving the restaurant they met the Ramley captain, Stuart Wilkins, and two other members of the team, who were on their way in. "Eat as much as you can, lads" Clive told them. "You need to build up your strength if you're going to get anywhere on Saturday."

Wilkins replied, "We could go without food for a fortnight and still be strong enough to beat you lot. How many matches have you won this season?"

"It'll be one more after Saturday," said Clive, moving away.

The Ramley captain was determined to get another dig in. "By the way, Clive, how many women have you got in the team this week?"

"Three fewer than you," was Clive's immediate retort. "See you Saturday, Stu." He and Pat left before any of the Ramley contingent could think of anything else to say.

In spite of the great rivalry between the two teams and villages and the continual quest for one-upmanship, no real animosity was involved. The baiting and bickering always stopped short of anything nasty or violent. Always, that is, until this year. For the first time anyone in either camp could remember, blows were

A Good Catch

struck. And that before the game had started.

Inevitably, Kevin was the Marwen player in the thick of it. He'd had a bad morning. The two others who shared a house with him had left early for a weekend trip to London and hadn't bothered to wash their breakfast dishes. They had just piled them in the sink, on top of the unwashed dishes from Friday night's meal. So Kevin had had to wash the lot himself, smashing two plates and a mug in the process.

Then he had gone to Swansea to buy a new jacket, only to find when he got there that he had left his wallet and credit cards in the house. He drove back jacketless and intended having a quick lunch before going down to the ground for the big game. His quick lunch was to consist of bacon, egg and chips. But the others had finished off the eggs for breakfast, the bacon had gone off and there was only one potato left. He had had to settle for beans on toast.

Yes, all in all, it had been a bad morning for Kevin and he wasn't in the best of moods when he parked his Lotus Elan +2 in the cricket club car park. His mood deteriorated even further when he was struck on the shoulder by a cricket ball. Some of the Ramley players who had arrived early were throwing a ball around and a careless throw, a genuine accident, had resulted in Kevin's being hit.

"Sorry, pal," said Stuart Wilkins as he picked up the ball. "We're just getting in some catching practice. Not that we really need it."

Kevin just glared at him, then walked on. He hadn't walked far when the ball hit the car. Kevin was very proud of that car, so this wouldn't have been an incident he'd have taken lightly even if he hadn't been in a bad mood. He returned to the car and checked that there was no damage, then he picked up the ball and threw it as far as he could away from the car park.

"What the hell did you do that for?" yelled Wilkins.

"If you want to play, keep away from the cars. Even the kids round here know that." Kevin started walking again. "But then the kids round here have got some intelligence."

The Ramley captain moved in front of Kevin. "I don't think I like your tone, laddie. And I think you should go and fetch our ball back."

Kevin look straight at him. Or rather, looked up at him. Wilkins was much taller than Kevin. And a lot heavier. But Kevin was not to be intimidated. In no time at all the two were brawling. The first contest of the day was under way—with Marwen very much second-best.

Two of the Ramley players who had earlier been throwing the ball around came over to separate the two combatants, though they did hold back long enough for their captain to inflict further punishment on the hapless Kevin. Some people came out of the clubhouse to see what was going on and it was then that the Ramley men stepped in to stop the fight. They pulled Wilkins up, leaving Kevin on the ground.

A young woman ran over from the clubhouse. She turned on the Ramley captain. "What do you think you're doing? A grown man fighting in the car park. If this is the sort of example you set your team, I'm glad I don't come and watch you playing often."

"He asked for it," sneered Wilkins.

"And you, of course, had to give it to him. Oh, clear off, Stuart! Go and hit your players with a bat or whatever you do before the start of a game."

Wilkins muttered something, but the woman wasn't listening. She had knelt down beside Kevin and was looking at the injuries to his face. Wilkins walked away with his team-mates.

There was blood pouring from either side of Kevin's mouth and his right cheek was slightly swollen. He would have quite a bruise to show for his performance. But there was no serious damage, other than to his pride.

Kevin wasn't even thinking of his injuries. He was looking at a vision. There was an angel kneeling beside him, an incredibly attractive angel. Long dark hair, brown eyes and the most enticing lips he'd ever seen. He hadn't known before that angels wore lipstick.

As the fuzziness cleared from his mind, he realised that this was no angel. This was a woman. And what a woman! Kevin thought to himself even losing a fight can have its compensations.

The woman took a handkerchief from her pocket and wiped the blood from Kevin's mouth and chin. "Shouldn't you pick on someone your own size?" she asked. When Kevin went to reply, she told him, "Don't talk now. Let me clear this mess up."

Having cleaned his face, she helped Kevin to his feet, then introduced herself. "I'm Catherine Wilkins. That was my husband you were... having a disagreement with."

"Oh." Kevin didn't know what to say.

"Don't worry about it," she said. "I'm having disagreements with him all the time. Though I think I come out of them better than you did."

"I'm sorry if I've embarrassed you or..."

"You haven't caused any embarrassment. It's that lump I'm married to that causes me embarrassment. Time and again." Before Kevin could say anything, Catherine added, "Now run along and see to that cheek of yours. Hold a cold, damp cloth or sponge against it for a while. It'll help draw out the bruise."

Before leaving her, Kevin said, "Thanks a lot for your help. I'm sorry we had to meet under such... awkward circumstances." He moved away, then turned back, "Perhaps I'll see you later on."

"I'll look forward to it. Now go on."

Kevin headed for the changing room. His mind was in a turmoil as he went. This woman was something special. He was certainly attracted to her and he sensed that she too was attracted to him. But she was married and he had always drawn the line at married women.

He had laid down that rule when he was fourteen after his mother had left home to live with another man. That had had a devastating effect on Kevin's father, who was never to be the same again. He was a broken man and though he always did his best for the children–Kevin and his elder sister–he had lost his previous vibrancy; his spirit had gone. Kevin had vowed then that he would never be the cause of such devastation, he would never get involved with a married woman. And he had stuck to that vow ever since.

His intention of sticking to it hadn't really been tested until now. But what a stern test this would be. Catherine was very attractive, very desirable and perhaps very willing. But she was married and he had always drawn the line at married women.

Still, she wasn't happily married. She herself had intimated as much. But the fact remained that she was married and he had always drawn the line at married women. Kevin wondered whether perhaps the time had come to redraw the line.

He reached the door of the changing room, then stopped and said, "Damn!" He remembered that he hadn't told her his name. In frustration and forgetting about his injuries, he leaned forward and banged his head against the door.

As he did so, Jessica came past. "There's no need to do that, Kev. Use the handle, it's quite easy."

* * *

Ramley won the toss and elected to bat. Within half an hour it looked as if they would regret that decision. At 33 for 4 they were in serious trouble.

The next man in was Stuart Wilkins. His side needed the proverbial 'captain's innings' from him now if they were to avoid an embarrassing result against their arch rivals. And a captain's innings he provided—with more than a little help from the arch rivals themselves.

Yes, the disease struck again. In spite of some extra training sessions called purely and simply to improve the catching, the side continued to spill catches at an alarming rate. Wilkins was dropped twice in his first ten minutes at the crease, once by Arthur behind the stumps and once by Clive at gully. He then grew in confidence and started to take the bowling apart. The opening bowlers gave way to an all-spin attack, Bob Evans at one end and John Price at the other.

The score had moved on to 102 before the next wicket fell. A superb throw to the wicket-keeper from Kevin at mid wicket as the batsmen went for a quick single resulted in a run-out. Kevin was well pleased with the throw, but was disappointed that it was the other batsman, not Wilkins, who was out. If he'd had time to think, he'd have thrown to the bowler's end instead. Then justice would have been done. That would have taught him a lesson.

Still, Kevin thought, there's plenty of time left and he's bound to make another mistake. In fact, he made three other mistakes, offering three more possible catching chances. Yet all of them were dropped, the third one by Kevin himself. It was a very difficult chance. Kevin was again at mid-wicket and Wilkins pulled the ball hard, slightly off the ground. Kevin dived to his right and got his hand to the ball but failed to hold it. He had saved an almost certain boundary and had made a chance out of a situation which wouldn't have been a chance for most. But that was no consolation for Kevin. He had missed an opportunity to get even.

Wilkins gave no more chances and went on to score a century. When he reached three figures everyone applauded–except Kevin. Wilkins noticed the snub and made a mental note that this young upstart would have to be taught another lesson soon.

One more wicket fell, but it wasn't Wilkins's. Andy Jones was the bowler and Arthur took a catch behind the wicket, much to his own delight. Arthur had said after his earlier miss that if he dropped another catch that day, he would throw away his gloves and keep wicket without them. Now at least the gloves could stay, for which Arthur's hands would be eternally grateful.

After 50 overs Ramley had scored 214 for 6. Bearing in mind their dreadful start, they were absolutely delighted. None more so than Stuart Wilkins, who was undefeated on 117. As he passed Kevin on his way from the field, he said "Hard lines, young man. That would have been some catch."

"There'll be other times," Kevin said.

"We'll have to wait and see about that, won't we." Wilkins moved on to acknowledge the applause of the spectators and his team-mates.

*   *   *

Ramley had made a bad start to their innings, but when Marwen batted their start was nothing short of disastrous., After six overs the score stood at 14 for 3. The first two wickets were the result of wild flashes outside the off-stump. Both catches were taken by the wicket-keeper. Clive was annoyed at his batsmen's recklessness. There was no need for such strokes so early in the innings.

Ian Cowling didn't make any rash strokes. In fact, when the last ball of the sixth over came down he didn't play any stroke at all, being prepared to just let the ball go through to the wicket-keeper. But the ball cut back from outside the off stump, hit Ian on the pad and he was given out l.b.w. Clive wasn't too pleased with that approach either.

So the score was 14 for 3 and defeat was staring Marwen in the face. And no ordinary defeat at that. If the innings continued as it had started, the end result would be complete humiliation for the team and the village.

Fortunately, the innings didn't continue as it had started and the rot was stopped. Kevin went in at No. 5 and he and Bob Evans set about taking the sting out of the Ramley bowling. They took no chances and just plodded on, taking any runs which came their way. They didn't go looking for big hits. All they did was wait for the bad balls and try to punish as many of those as they could.

The longer the two stayed at the crease, the more frustrated the bowlers became and the more frequently the bad balls came down. Stuart Wilkins, in particular, was feeling frustrated. Having opened the bowling, he had taken two wickets and when he saw Kevin coming to the middle, he couldn't wait to get at this arrogant upstart.

As things turned out, however, he hardly had a chance to get at him. It was almost always Bob who was facing him and Wilkins just couldn't get Kevin down the batting end on his overs. At one stage he even changed the bowling around in order to bring himself on at the other end. But in the meantime the batsmen had changed ends too, so when Wilkins came on to bowl, there was Bob waiting for him and with neither a single nor a three being scored Bob was still down there at the end of the over. Wilkins

A Good Catch

growled as he walked away.

The 50 partnership came up and the situation seemed to be improving for Marwen. It must have been improving because T.G., who had taken refuge in the bar when the early wickets fell, had now come out to sit on one of the benches near the boundary.

It wasn't long, however, before he was back in the bar drowning his sorrows again. From 65 for 3 Marwen slipped to 65 for 5, with both Bob and Kevin back in the changing room.

Neither of them was happy with his dismissal–and with good reason, for in actual fact neither of them was really out. Bob lost his wicket as a result of a "con" job on the umpire. Seeing little likelihood of separating the fourth-wicket pair, the Ramley players decided to appeal loudly and strongly whenever the ball hit a batsman's pad, irrespective of whether they thought he was out or not.

Wilkins was still bowling and when he started a new over, the first ball cut back very sharply and hit Bob on the pad. It was obvious that the ball would have missed leg stump by some way, yet the Ramley players yelled, almost in unison, "Owzthat!". The young umpire, in only his second season in the league, shook his head, Wilkins looked at him questioningly.

"Missing leg stick," the umpire said.

Now it was Wilkins who was shaking his head.

"I don't believe it," the mid-off fielder told his captain as the latter walked back to his mark. The fielder spoke loudly enough for the umpire to hear. "No way was that missing the stumps. No way. You should complain. He's too young to umpire a game like this."

"Leave it, said Wilkins. "We all make mistakes."

There was no mistake, the umpire thought to himself. He was certain that he was right. Well, almost certain. Would the ball have hit the stumps? Did he have a momentary lapse of concentration which caused him to miss what everyone else could see? Perhaps that was it. It didn't usually happen to him, but it could happen to anyone. Anyway, whatever had happened, the decision had been given and it was final–though he hoped that if a mistake had been made, the batsman wouldn't stay in too long and make it a costly one.

The fifth ball of the over hit Bob high on the pad. It would almost certainly have gone over the top of the stumps. But that didn't stop the Ramley players appealing again even more confidently than before. As they yelled, they looked at the umpire expectantly. He thought the ball would have missed the stumps. Or would it? There was a confident shout. Really confident. Perhaps the ball would have hit the wicket. High up perhaps, but a hit nevertheless. Yes, it would have hit it. No question about it. The umpire raised his finger.

Bob looked at him in amazement. He couldn't believe it. The oldest trick in the book and the umpire had fallen for it. But there was nothing Bob could do. The decision had been made. He had been given out and that was that. He made his way to the changing room.

Wilkins was over the moon. The breakthrough had been made and the way was open for victory over the old enemy. He had taken his third wicket and the match was becoming an exceedingly good one for him personally.

He was even more pleased in the next over as he was to have a hand in Kevin's dismissal. Two hands actually. He was fielding near the young umpire at square-leg when Kevin received a difficult rising delivery and played it down the leg side. Wilkins dived forward to try and catch the ball before it hit the ground. He scooped the ball up in his hands, but this was after it had hit the ground. Still, it was only a split second after, so it would be worth appealing.

Appeal he did, along with the rest of his team. The young umpire at square-leg didn't see what happened, as he was standing behind the diving Wilkins. The other umpire thought it was a catch but wasn't sure. He asked the Ramley captain whether the ball had touched the ground and Wilkins assured him that it hadn't. The umpire raised his finger.

Kevin was furious. He knew it wasn't a catch. And he knew that Wilkins knew it wasn't a catch. "You bastard!" he told Wilkins as he walked past him. "You knew damn well it was grounded."

Wilkins smiled and said, "All's fair in love and cricket."

So Bob and Kevin had ample cause to feel aggrieved. But the fact remained that Marwen were 65 for 5 and in deep trouble.

Clive and Jessica were at the crease and the captain told his batting partner to curb her natural inclination to go for runs. The team had no hope of winning the match, their only chance of saving face was to hold out for a draw. There were still 28 overs to go, so they had a lot to do.

By the time the number of overs had gone down to twenty, both Clive and Jessica had been dismissed and had left the field of play. Jessica was changing in the ladies' toilet and Clive had stayed outside to watch the remainder of the match. The scoreboard made for miserable reading. Marwen were 72 for 7.

Clive had taken off his pads and was sitting on a bench, looking round the ground. This was not to be a happy day in the history of Marwen Cricket Club. Not only would they lose to their local rivals, but they would do so in a totally undignified manner. They had failed even to make a game of it. Apart from the first half hour of the match, they had been completely outplayed. They would lose by over a hundred runs, unless the remaining batsmen could hold out for the last twenty overs. But there was little chance of that. Even less chance now. Barry Roberts had just been caught behind the wicket. 72 for 8.

Arthur made his way to the crease to partner John Price. The only other batsman left was Andy Jones. It was very unlikely that these three between them could hold out for twenty overs. Not one of them was renowned for his batting prowess.

Arthur safely played out the remainder of the over. Nineteen overs to go.

Clive again took in the view. The sight of what was going on in the middle might not be pleasant, but the ground itself was always worth looking at. He had looked around this ground many times over the years, but never ceased to be struck by the beauty of the view. It was especially beautiful in the sunshine. There was no sunshine now. In fact, it was quite cloudy. But when the sun did shine on the ground, it was...

Clive's thoughts stopped suddenly. What had his mind just registered. He thought back. "There was no sunshine now... it was quite cloudy." He looked up. It was indeed cloudy. The clouds right above the ground were high and held little hope of rain, but in the distance Clive could see darker clouds moving in from the west, and those most definitely were rain clouds.

Could there yet be hope? Clive kept looking towards John and when he caught his eye he pointed in the direction of the incoming clouds. John looked to see what Clive was pointing at and understood immediately.

Stuart Wilkins had also noticed the threatening clouds and called on his team for one last effort to finish off the opposition quickly.

John was in no such hurry. He would now do all he could to delay matters and prolong the match. He took fresh guard after every other ball. He then stopped the game so that he could adjust one of his pads. It had slipped round and would hinder his running, he told the fuming Ramley skipper.

"You lot aren't doing any running," Wilkins replied. "You're only holding out for a draw."

John smiled and thought to himself, "I'll be running pretty fast when that rain starts, pal."

Another over was completed and by now the dark clouds were almost above them. The rain itself didn't start until the middle of the next over and when it did start the reactions of the opposing captains were quite different. It was all that Clive could do to restrain himself from jumping off the bench and punching the air in celebratory fashion. Wilkins, on the other hand, was seething. Fielding at mid-on, he threw the ball to the bowler and told him to put all he had into this over to try to finish off the innings.

The bowler didn't get a chance to comply with his captain's instructions. Arthur held up proceedings to tie one of his laces and by the time he had picked up his bat again the rain was falling steadily. The umpire suggested that perhaps they should go off until the rain eased a little, but Wilkins emphatically rejected the suggestion. "It's not raining that much," he said. "We're quite prepared to carry on."

"What about the batsmen?" the umpire asked John, who was down at the non-striking end.

"No way," John replied instantly. "We're not batting in this. It's too dangerous. We don't want anybody getting injured without need."

The umpire nodded and off they came, despite Wilkins's vociferous protests. The question now was: Would the rain continue long enough to prevent any further play? For every three minutes the players were off, an over was lost. When they came off there were seventeen full overs to go in addition to the three remaining deliveries of the uncompleted over.

Clive kept an eye on his watch, counting off the overs as each three minutes went by. Stuart Wilkins paced up and down the corridor outside the changing rooms. No-one went near him. They knew the safest thing to do was to keep well clear.

Half an hour went by. Or more to the point, ten overs were lost. There would be only seven and a half overs at most for Ramley to take the remaining wickets. The rain had eased slightly, but was still falling. Wilkins opened the door to the Marwen team's changing room. "Are you prepared to go out now?" he asked.

John Price stood on the bench which ran along the far wall and looked through the window which was set in the upper part of the wall. "It's still raining," he said.

"Not much," Wilkins asserted.

"Too much for me," John said as he got down from the bench.

Wilkins slammed the door behind him when he left. The Marwen players burst into laughter.

The rain continued for another hour. The match was drawn. Everyone knew that Marwen had been outplayed on the day, but the record books would show that they hadn't lost. And that was good enough for the people of Marwen. Their team would have the opportunity to put in a better performance when the two teams met again at Ramley in the second half of the season.

* * *

After showering and changing, both teams settled down in the bar for a few drinks together now that the tensions of the match were behind them. They joked about the game. The Ramley players pointed out that were it not for the rain they would have won easily. John and Arthur, on the other hand, pointed out that at the very least they would have held out for a draw, but they might even have decided to go for the runs and win the match.

"You'd have had to go at eight runs an over," one of the Ramley players said.

"So?" John said. "There was nothing in the bowling. Eight runs an over would have been no problem for us. Would it, Arthur?"

Everyone laughed and after some further analysis of today's game and the season in general, they moved on to talk about other things—and the drinks went down steadily.

Only two of the players were not enjoying the evening. One was the Ramley captain, still furious at Marwen's refusal to continue the game when it was so near completion.

Clive told him, "Surely you didn't expect us to just give you the points, Stu."

"The sporting thing to do would have been to carry on with the game," said Wilkins.

Clive then finished off the discussion. "Listen, Stu, we both know what you'd have done had the positions been reversed."

To that there was no answer. Stuart Wilkins knew full well that he would have done exactly the same. In fact, he had done so two seasons previously in a match at Brynteg. But this was different. This was unsporting. He sat, simmering quietly for most of the evening, rarely joining in the conversation and when he did it was invariably with some barbed comment.

The other player not enjoying the evening was Kevin. He had been looking forward to talking again to the attractive Catherine, but he didn't get the chance. She had been sitting all evening at a table with her husband, Clive and Pat. Kevin didn't go anywhere near the table as he knew he couldn't be civil to Wilkins.

He had a few pints with the rest of the lads, but didn't really join in the spirit of the proceedings. He kept glancing over at Catherine. Their eyes did meet once, but almost immediately Wilkins said something to his wife and the contact was broken.

Kevin thought back over the events of the day and noted how time and again Wilkins had managed to spoil things for him. And he was still doing it now. Kevin didn't feel like staying here any longer. A day he had been looking forward to for some time had gone wrong from the start, so the best thing to do was go home, have an early night and start again tomorrow. He finished his drink, said his goodbyes and left.

Things continued to go wrong in the car park. As he was going to open the door of the car, he dropped the keys and couldn't see them in the dim light. He had to go down on his knees to look for them. He then got up and opened the door.

"How's the cheek?" a voice behind him asked.

He turned and saw Catherine approaching him. "It's OK, thanks," he replied.

"You're leaving early," she said. "I thought everyone stayed to have a good night after these local derbies, or whatever you call them."

"They do usually. And I do usually. I just don't feel like it tonight."

"I know what you mean. I wish I could get away too. But... well, captain's wife and all that."

Kevin nodded, then looked at her quietly for a moment. This was certainly one of the most beautiful women he'd ever met. Even in that dim light her face was radiant. "Oh, by the way," he said, "I haven't introduced myself. I'm Kevin."

"I know."

Kevin looked surprised.

"Yes, I've been checking up on you."

"Find out anything interesting?"

"Mm. Quite a bit. Perhaps I'll tell you some time."

Kevin again sensed that if he made a move she'd be responsive. "I'd been hoping to talk to you earlier, to thank you for your help this afternoon. But I didn't seem to get a chance. You were with your husband all the time and . . . well, he and I aren't on the best of terms."

"He and I aren't either. All that devoted wife stuff in there is just an act. Keeping up appearances."

"Problems?"

"Plenty. That's why I'm going away for a few days. On my own. To sort things out more clearly in my mind. After that . . . " She shrugged her shoulders.

Kevin was disappointed to hear that she was going away. He was hoping they could have gone out together some time soon. Catherine sensed his disappointment and told him, "I'll only be gone for a few days. I'll be back by the end of the week." She started to move off.

"I'd better go back in before they miss me. I'll phone you when I get back."

"I'd better give you my number."

"No need. I've already got it. I told you, I've been checking up on you."

And then she was gone. Kevin got into his car and drove off. He was in a much happier frame of mind now. So the day hadn't been a total disaster. She really was interested in him. But again the doubts came. She was a married woman and he had always kept clear of married women. How could she have married that pillock? What could she have seen in him? Whatever the reason, she had married him. Whatever their problems, she was still married to him. And seeing as they were having problems, shouldn't he, Kevin, keep out of it rather than complicate matters?

Yet, it was obvious that she wanted involvement with Kevin. And he certainly was attracted to her. So what was the problem? After all, in Wilkins's own words, "All's fair in love and cricket."

Kevin arrived home, all his doubts dispelled.

Chapter 6

A SUMMER BREAK

At their next meeting the members of Marwen's committee were in a rather subdued mood. They all knew that the season was going very badly for them. They all knew that the hoped-for boost to confidence that would have followed a good performance in the local derby would not now materialise. They all knew that relegation was staring them in the face.

Something had to be done. But what? Some of the players would show glimpses of form, but only glimpses. There was no consistency other than consistently bad results for the team as a whole. An injection of new blood was needed from somewhere, and it was needed soon. It wouldn't come from the second team because that was made up almost entirely of youngsters not yet ready for the first team.

Clive informed the committee that he had spoken to his brother over the phone a couple of times during the week and had been told yesterday that the Australian he had mentioned at a previous committee meeting, the one who wanted to play cricket in Britain, would soon be on his way and was interested in coming to Marwen. He should be arriving at Heathrow early next week.

"How much is it going to cost us?" Doc asked. As treasurer, this was of prime concern to him.

"Apparently, if we provide lodgings for him and give him some beer money, he'll leave it at that."

Doc replied instantly, "Have you seen how much Australians drink?"

Clive put the treasurer's mind at rest. "Leave him to me, Doc. He'll stay with us and be well fed. He'll know that he's being treated well. Give him a few quid in his pocket and that should do it. According to my brother, he's not short of money. Far from it, apparently."

"In that case," Doc said, "perhaps he can pass some of his money on to us."

"It's more important that he passes some of his expertise on to us," Clive retorted.

"Isn't it just," T.G. exclaimed. "We need that far more than money. I don't relish going down to the Third Division, thank you very much. It'd be humiliating."

"And to think," Doc said, "before the start of the season we were considering our chances of going up to the First."

No-one chuckled, no-one smiled even. Despondency was the order of the day.

When it came to selecting the team for the next fixture, away to Tresarn, they decided to make one change, bringing in Pete Richards in place of Barry Roberts. Pete hadn't played since failing to turn up for the game at Choreton owing to his having gone to the hospital to witness the birth of his first child. Barry, on the other hand, was having a bad time with the bat, and in spite of being moved down the batting order just couldn't get many runs.

The committee felt that bringing Pete back would strengthen the batting a little and they hoped that this change, together with the Australian's arrival the following week, would enable an upturn in the club's fortunes. Little did they know that, far from experiencing an upturn, the club's fortunes were to take a nose-dive during the game at Tresarn.

* * *

Tresarn batted first and subjected the Marwen players to a torrid time in the field. And the Marwen players didn't help matters much with their apparent determination to drop any catches that came their way.

Three catches went down in the first seven overs. John Price dropped a difficult chance while fielding at gully, Bob dropped one at mid-on and Kevin was the other culprit. Clive had decided to try Kevin back in the slips, hoping that by now his confidence would have returned. But when the chance came, he reacted too slowly and the catch was dropped. He moved out of the slips at the end of the over, vowing never to return as long as he lived.

The dropped catches proved very costly indeed. The Tresarn opening batsmen recovered from their shaky start and gave no more chances. They took plenty of time to play themselves in and then began to get on top of the bowling. The 50 came up in the eighteenth over, but then the batsmen seemed to cut loose and the ball was dispatched to all parts of the ground. They took only eight overs to score the next 50 and after thirty overs the score had moved on to 134 without loss. There was nothing Marwen could do about it. Clive changed the bowling around, but nothing seemed to work. The runs just kept on flowing.

As if that wasn't enough, catastrophe then befell the Marwen team—and Bob in particular. He was fielding at mid-wicket. The batsman played the ball to the on-side and called for a quick single. Bob ran in quickly to try to effect a run-out, but as he stooped to pick up the ball his foot twisted and he fell awkwardly on his right arm.

It was obvious at once that something was wrong and the Marwen players ran over to Bob. He was having a great deal of pain near his right ankle and a sprain seemed likely. He was also having a little discomfort from his arm, but the ankle seemed to be the main problem.

The Tresarn captain brought out a glass of water for Bob, who drank it and then wanted to get to his feet. He was helped up, but his leg gave way almost immediately. Kevin and Clive carried him off and put him in a chair on the edge of the boundary.

"Just give me a few minutes, "Bob said, "then I'll come back."

Clive and Kevin looked at one another. Neither thought that

Bob would take any further part in the game. They left him and returned to the field of play.

The only good thing to come from the incident from Marwen's point of view was that it broke the batsmen's concentration. Within two overs both were out, one bowled by John Price, the other l.b.w. to Pete Richards, who had been brought on earlier to try to break the stand with his medium-pace bowling. That Pete was bowling showed how desperate the situation had become.

Unfortunately for Marwen, the fall of the two wickets proved to be only a temporary respite and the fielders were soon chasing the ball to all parts of the ground again. When forty overs had been completed, the score was 176 for 2.

The stage was now set for Tresarn to hit out over the last ten overs and amass a really big score. Four batting points had already been secured and if the batsmen succeeded in their hitting out another two could be gained. The score went well beyond the 200. As the batsmen chased the runs in a cavalier fashion, the pressure on the fielders was increased. It was quite ironic, therefore, that under this pressure the catching improved and three catches were taken from the next three chances.

Two of the catches were taken by Andy Jones on the long-on boundary. On both occasions the ball was hit hard and high, and on both occasions Andy did everything right, positioning himself correctly, keeping his eye on the ball and taking the catch.

As well as the catches there had been a run-out and by the time the last ball was to be bowled the score was 239 for 6. One more run was needed for a sixth batting point. The ball was again hit high towards the long-on boundary, Andy was again the fielder waiting for it. Whereas on the two previous occasions the others hadn't expected him to take the catch, they now fully expected him to do so; whereas on the two previous occasions he himself hadn't expected to take the catch, he now expected to do so. Whereas on the two previous occasions he had taken the catch, he now failed to do so. The disease was back. Tresarn's innings closed on 241 for 6.

Although Bob hadn't been able to return to the field, he had been able, after a while, to put his weight on the right ankle. He was able to move around, albeit with a limp, and this was a welcome sight for the rest of the team as they left the field after a long, hard stint.

Clive was glad to see that Bob's injury wasn't as bad as it had at first appeared. Perhaps he might even be able to bat. They would certainly need his batting expertise if they were to avoid defeat.

What Clive didn't know was that, while Bob's ankle injury wasn't so serious, the injury to his right arm was very serious indeed. Bob had continued to feel discomfort in the arm and by now he was unable to move his fingers freely. When Bob told Clive about this, the captain replied, "You know what that could mean."

"A break."

"Quite possibly. We'll get you to the hospital as soon as we can."

"Damn!" Bob said and kicked the chair he had been sitting on. Which was a stupid thing to do, because he kicked it with his right foot. Now the ankle was playing up again.

Clive put Bob to sit down and ordered him to stay put. It was decided not to give him any food in case it would cause problems when it came to having treatment at the hospital.

Clive told Kevin to open the batting instead of Bob, then as soon as he lost his wicket, he was to take Bob to the nearest hospital, in Swansea. Not that that meant, Clive added, that Kevin was to throw his wicket away. He was to stay at the crease for as long as he could. Which, of course, was Kevin's intention. He wanted to bat for as long as possible and score as much as possible–as he told Clive after being bowled by the last ball of the first over.

Kevin changed quickly, then brought the car round to pick up Bob. Bob got into the car very carefully and Kevin drove off. As they left the ground, the scoreboard read 15 for 2.

When they arrived at the hospital, the first person they met was Catherine Wilkins. She was a Sister on duty in the A&E Department. Kevin felt like thanking Bob for breaking his arm.

"What are you doing here?" Catherine asked.

"I've brought him in," answered Kevin, pointing to Bob. "He felt like seeing the inside of a hospital, so he fell on his arm during today's game."

Bob said nothing, he just smiled. Catherine told him to go with her. Kevin followed them, talking as he went. "Mind you, if I'd known you were here tonight and he hadn't fallen I'd have been tempted to fall on my arm." They reached one of the treatment rooms and Kevin was still talking. "Or on second thoughts, I'd have pushed him so that he'd fall on his arm."

Catherine turned and, guiding Kevin out of the treatment room, said, "Be quiet, Kevin, and go back to the waiting room. Give us a chance to see to him."

Kevin looked at her, then shrugged his shoulders. "OK. I know where I'm not wanted." He started back towards the waiting room, then turned. "Take good care of him. He's our best player." He walked on a little further, then turned again. "Scratch that last remark. He's our second-best player." He straightened his shoulder and continued his way to the waiting room.

Catherine smiled at Kevin's jabbering. When he was finally gone, she went back into the treatment room to Bob. What she didn't realise was that Kevin's babbling was due to nervousness at being in a hospital. He disliked hospitals and always felt uncomfortable in one.

After being examined by the doctor in A&E Bob was taken to the X-ray Department. When he returned to the doctor after the latter had had a chance to look at the X-rays, he was told that there was indeed a break, a collis fracture. The arm would have to be reset. Not immediately, however, because an ambulance had just arrived bringing in a road accident victim. The doctor and Catherine left Bob in the treatment room.

After about ten minutes Catherine came back. "Sorry for the delay, Bob. A little boy's been knocked down. He's not too bad, but we have to see to him first. So if you can hang on a little longer."

Bob said, "I'll have to use my left arm to do that."

Catherine looked at him bemused, then realised the joke. She smiled. More out of sympathy than amusement, Bob thought. She asked, "Shall I send Kevin in to keep you company?"

"No thanks," Bob replied immediately. "I've got enough problems."

Catherine smiled again, then left. It was over twenty minutes before she returned with the doctor. In next-to-no-time the arm was re-set, the plaster put on and the arm put in a sling. Bob was taken to another room to recover. He was put on a bed, then Catherine lifted the rails on either side of the bed. "Just a precaution," she told Bob. "You're still a little drowsy after the injection and we don't want you falling out of bed. You might break your arm or something." Bob smiled.

Having given the patient time to recover, Catherine brought Kevin in to see him. She warned Bob not to eat much that night and not to drink any alcohol. Kevin said, "If that's what happens, I must remember never to break my arm."

Bob was given some pain-killing tablets to take every four hours and told to come back on the Monday to make sure everything was alright.

"How are you going to manage tonight?" Catherine asked him. He had told her earlier that he lived alone.

"He can sleep with me tonight," Kevin said.

"Oh, there's nice!" exclaimed Catherine.

"I didn't mean it like that."

Catherine laughed.

Bob assured them he'd be alright in his own home. "You're just round the corner, Kev. If I need anything I'll phone and you'll be round in no time." It took a little while for Bob to convince Kevin, but in the end he succeeded. And now they could leave.

"See you tomorrow," Kevin whispered to Catherine as he went past her. Via phone calls earlier in the day, they had arranged to go out together on the Sunday afternoon. She wouldn't be working until the night and her husband would be away playing cricket in a cup match.

* * *

Meanwhile, back at Tresarn, the Marwen players were changing after what had been for them another disastrous game. Their innings had started badly and never improved. Wickets had fallen steadily and the attainment of double figures seemed to be an objective beyond the capabilities of the players. Only Clive and Ian Cowling attained that objective, the others got nowhere near.

The aim, almost from the outset, was to hold out for a draw. Between them, the batsmen had to survive fifty overs. As it turned out, the last wicket fell in the 34th over with the total a miserable 69. It wouldn't even have been that much had not the Tresarn wicket-keeper had an off day and conceded 21 byes.

The mood in the Marwen changing room after the game was one of total depression. There was nothing that could be said to lift the gloom. They had been completely outplayed for the second successive Saturday and the hopes of an improvement which had been kindled a few weeks earlier had now been totally extinguished. The halfway stage of the season had been reached and when the League table would be published following today's results, it would show Marwen firmly rooted to the bottom. They would now have to play again all the teams that had trounced them in the first half of the season—and they would have to play them without Bob. Little wonder then that the players were depressed.

Arthur tried to raise their spirits. "Cheer up, lads. That's the first half of the season gone and good riddance to it. Now for the second half. Things can only get better."

"Without Bob?" Ian commented. "You've got to be joking. Let's face it. The second half of the season will probably be even worse than the first."

"That's a defeatist attitude," said Arthur. "Think positive, man."

"OK. The second half of the season will definitely be worse than the first."

The others didn't laugh, simply nodding their agreement with what they regarded as a valid statement. Arthur gave up. He had finished changing, so he headed for the bar to talk to the Tresarn players. They were bound to be better company.

A Good Catch

Before long the other Marwen players followed. They stayed in the bar for about half an hour, then left to drown their sorrows in their own village.

* * *

Also on their way back to Marwen were Kevin and Bob. But they were travelling more slowly. Much more slowly. Bob had put himself as comfortable as he could in Kevin's Lotus. He rested his arm against his body and asked Kevin not to hit any pot-holes if at all possible.

"Don't worry," Kevin told him. "I'll drive slowly. You won't even know we're moving."

And he kept his word. He didn't move out of third gear. Soon Bob had to laugh. "You can go faster than this, Kev. I don't want any more pedestrians walking past us."

Kevin took the hint and moved up the gears. He kept a keen eye open for any bumps in the road and managed to avoid all the pot-holes, which was no mean feat considering the state of the roads in the area.

"Do you want to go straight home?" Kevin asked.

"No, I'd better go to Carol's to break... to tell her the news. I suppose in a way she'll be pleased. She's been getting more and more annoyed lately about the cricket taking me away every Saturday. Now she'll think that problem's gone."

"You'll still be coming down to watch us, won't you?"

"Of course I will. But Carol doesn't know that. And when she finds out, a broken arm will be the least of my problems."

As they neared Marwen, Kevin laughed and when Bob asked him why, he said, "I was just wondering about you and Carol... How you'll manage... You know."

Bob sighed. "Look, Kev, don't think up any more problems for me. Let me take them one at a time."

Kevin laughed again.

"What now?" Bob asked.

"I was just thinking you're going to have to be satisfied with a bit of armless fun."

Bob sighed again. What had he done to deserve a friend like Kevin?

* * *

Carol Treharne lived with her parents in Marwen. She was twenty-four years old and worked in a building society office in Swansea, but had no great career aspirations. Her main ambition was to marry Bob and raise a family. A number of her friends berated her for setting her sights so low and told her she could have a family and a good career. She just ignored them. Let's see who'll be happiest in thirty years' time, she thought to herself.

The two had been going steady for over two years, but Bob still hadn't popped the question. Carol had tried to get him to do so but had failed thus far. Bob admitted they would get married eventually, but he wasn't ready yet. He had qualified as a solicitor just before starting to go out with Carol and he wanted to secure his professional future before taking on further responsibilities.

Carol had told him that his professional future was secure. He had been taken on almost immediately by a firm of solicitors in Carmarthen and they were well satisfied with him. There was every likelihood that he would be offered a partnership with them. But Bob still wanted to wait. "One partnership at a time," he would say.

What Carol didn't know was that Bob had already been offered a partnership and had accepted. He had kept quiet about it, knowing that once he told Carol she would be on at him even more about getting engaged. And he didn't want to be pressured into that.

With Bob standing just behind him, Kevin rang the doorbell of the Treharne home. Carol herself answered. She looked at Bob in amazement. "What on earth?"

"I've broken my arm, babe," said Bob.

"How?"

"In the game this afternoon."

"I should've known. I've told you often enough you shouldn't play that stupid game. Perhaps now you'll listen."

"OK, I give in. I won't play next week."

A Good Catch

Kevin then stepped in. "But he has said he'll be available the following week."

Carol looked at Kevin, horrified. Then she turned to Bob and was about to say something when the two men laughed. Carol took everybody so seriously.

They went into the house. Carol's parents were out for the evening. Carol was given a full account of the accident and she wasn't too impressed. Kevin stayed for about ten minutes, then excused himself. "I'll go down the club to see the lads. Reassure them that you're going to live."

"You don't have to go," Bob said.

"Yes, I do. Remember, I'm not the one who's supposed to leave off alcohol."

Carol showed Kevin out, then came back to sit next to Bob on the sofa. "Are you alright?" she asked.

"Yes," he said. "I'll be as right as rain in a couple of weeks." He felt some pain in his arm and his face showed this. He saw that Carol had noticed, so he added, "Well, perhaps a little longer."

They sat and talked for a while, then Carol made some coffee for them both. "I suppose there's some good even from an accident like this," she said as she sat down after bringing in the coffee.

"What do you mean?" Bob asked.

"Well, we've been talking for a while here now and haven't argued once about cricket." Bob said nothing and Carol went on. "And we'll be able to spend our Saturdays together now. You know I've always wanted that."

Now Bob did step in. "Hang on now, babe. I may not be able to play, but I'll still be going down to the games." He ignored the look of total surprise on Carol's face. "To support them. To help them."

"How can you help them with a broken arm."

"If they need an umpire, I can do that. Or I can help behind the bar somehow. Or..."

They were soon quarrelling about cricket again. Perhaps the accident hadn't changed matters much after all.

* * *

By the time Kevin arrived at the clubhouse, the others were well on their way to drowning their sorrows. He gave them a full account of Bob's time at the hospital and they gave him a much briefer account of the game.

Ian remarked, "Our team's in a worse state than Bob's arm. At least Bob's arm is going to get better."

Kevin looked at the downcast faces around the table. "Have you lot been like this ever since the game?"

"And how!" Arthur exclaimed. "They've already resigned themselves to relegation."

"Well, we'll have to do something about that," Kevin said. Having noticed that all the glasses on the table were over half-full, he asked, "Anybody need a drink? No? . . . OK then, hang on while I get one for myself."

As he got to the bar, T.G. joined him. "Mine's a whisky, Kev."

Kevin laughed. "I wondered where you'd got to." he ordered the drinks, then told the chairman about Bob.

T.G. had obviously had quite a few whiskies already and the confirmation of the fears about Bob's arm almost brought tears to his eyes. "I was hoping against hope that it wasn't broken. But there wasn't really much doubt, was there." He shook his head. "I don't know how we're going to manage without him."

"Cheer up, T.G." Kevin said. "You've still got me."

The chairman looked at Kevin, then ordered another whisky.

Kevin rejoined the others and sat next to Clive. "Well, skip, I'm assuming that you're looking at things more positively. After all, you are our leader."

But even the leader was dejected. "It's looking bad, Kev. I don't know how we're going to get out of this mess. At first I thought it was just a matter of waiting for players to get their form back. But we've waited and waited and we're still waiting. Then Bob's injury on top of everything. It's as if everything's going against us."

"Not everything, skip. The Australian arrives next week. Perhaps he'll improve things."

"What can one man do?"

"We'll have to wait and see on that. But at least it's one glimmer of hope."

"The only one, Kev."

"Oh, come on skip, it's not like you to be down like this. You're usually the one to pick everybody else up. It's getting to be like a morgue in here."

Clive looked at Kevin for a moment, then nodded. "You're right, Kev. Talk like this'll get us nowhere. Especially coming from the captain." He got up. "Right, let's have another drink." He picked up his own glass and Kevin's and asked if anyone else wanted a drink. No-one did, so he went to the bar.

"Mine's a whisky," said a voice to his right.

* * *

Carol drove Bob home shortly after eleven o' clock. She had asked him to stay at her house so that there'd be somebody to look after him if anything went wrong, but Bob had insisted on going home. "If I'm going to die, I'd rather die there." Noticing the look of alarm on Carol's face, he added, "I was only joking." She really did take everything seriously.

Carol was going to get out of the car, but Bob told her he'd be alright. They kissed, then he got out by himself. She said she'd call round first thing in the morning, then drove off. Bob was glad she didn't stay any longer. The pain was worse now and he wanted to take the tablets. Given Carol's tendency to fear the worst, that was best left until he was alone.

Letting himself into the house was no problem, but after that Bob discovered more and more how awkward life was going to be during the next few weeks. Everything would now have to be done with one arm, his left arm. Tasks which hitherto had been undertaken without thought now became matters of concentrated effort. Even pouring a glass of water became a marathon exercise. First of all, he had to reach for the glass with his left hand, then put the glass down. Turn on the tap. Pick up the glass and fill it. Put the glass down. Turn off the tap. Pick up the glass again and drink the water. Was it worth the effort?

Undressing was the next problem, but Bob thought of an easy

way round that. He would lie on the bed fully clad. He managed to untie his shoe-laces and take off his shoes. Then he lay on the bed, resting his right arm on the pillow he had pulled down to his side. He hoped he wouldn't turn over on his arm in his sleep, presuming that is that he would get any sleep.

As it turned out, he got more sleep than he'd expected and didn't once turn on his arm. But he was still glad when the morning came and it was time to get up. He looked at his shoes on the floor and realised that even putting those on would be beyond him now. How could he tie laces with one arm? He put his slippers on. The shoe problem could wait until Carol came.

Breakfast was another problem. He managed to have a bowl of corn flakes and a cup of tea. But as for bacon and eggs, which he liked to have every morning, that too would have to wait until Carol came.

Bob sat at the table, feeling very sorry for himself. Why had he bothered rushing for that ball? He wouldn't have prevented the single anyway. It was all so stupid and unnecessary. Well, now he was paying for that stupidity–and would be paying for it for some time to come. He'd have to depend on others for so much during the coming days and weeks. The more he thought of things he wouldn't be able to do for himself, the more depressed he became. He sighed. This was one summer break he certainly didn't appreciate.

Chapter 7

WALTZING MATILDA

There were no smiles at the following Monday's committee meeting. Little wonder. They had nothing to smile about. The team was firmly entrenched at the bottom of the table and their best player would be out of action for the remainder of the season. Relegation was a very real possibility.

T.G.'s previous sympathy regarding Bob's injury had by now turned to anger. "If he'd broken his arm while facing a really fast bowler, OK. But to slip while he was fielding..." He sighed and shook his head. "Had he been drinking?"

"You know better than to ask that," Clive said immediately. "It was an accident. Nothing more, nothing less. We've just got to accept it and do the best we can without him."

The chairman came back at him. "In other words, we've just got to accept relegation... 'cos that's where we're headed. No question about it."

Before Clive had a chance to reply, Arthur spoke. "Come on, T.G., we're not down yet and we should stop taking as if we were. If we give up now, we deserve to go down. There's still hope, provided we go on fighting."

T.G. wasn't convinced. "As Custer probably said at Little Big Horn."

"But no reinforcements arrived in time to help Custer," Arthur retorted. "Our reinforcements arrive this week. The Australian cavalry is on its way."

"You expect one Australian to change the fortunes of the whole team?"

"Why not? If he's any good, and Clive's brother says he is, he may be just the spur the other players need. He may bring the best out of them."

T.G. sniggered, "We've already seen their best. That's why we're bottom of the League."

"That's not fair," said Clive, coming to his team's defence. "We haven't seen their best this season. But, as Arthur said, there's still time. They've got the potential to be a good team."

"The only potential they've got is to be a relegated team. Look at our position in the table."

"But if..."

"No buts. Let's just face facts. Bob Evans is our best player and he's broken his arm. Though, come to think of it, he's probably still our best player, even with a broken arm."

Clive groaned. "There's no point talking like that, T.G. And there's no point going on and on about Bob. He's out for the season. He can't get us out of this mess. The others might. And the Australian of course. Arthur's right. He might make the world of a difference."

"We might make the world of a difference to him. Perhaps we'll pull him down to our level."

Clive sighed with exasperation, but Doc now intervened. He had allowed T.G. to let off steam for a while. That was necessary, as the chairman had been simmering since Saturday. But enough was enough. There was now need for sensible talk, positive decisions. "Alright," the treasurer said. "Let's cut out the wisecracks and start making decisions. That's what we're here for. We've got a team to pick for Saturday."

Doc's intervention was a welcome one because until then the meeting was getting nowhere. Glyn asked Clive whether the Australian definitely would be there to play on Saturday.

Clive nodded. "He should be. His plane arrived this morning and he phoned me to say he was staying with friends in London

A Good Catch

tonight, then coming down to us tomorrow. Pat and I'll go to Swansea to meet him from the train."

"Good," said Doc. "At least that seems to be going right. Now then, Saturday's team. The Australian will take Bob's place. Any more changes needed?"

"Ten," said the chairman, but everyone ignored the remark.

Glyn reminded the others that Barry had scored an excellent century for the second team on Saturday, so he might be in line for a quick recall. This was the first century of the season for any Marwen player. Everyone on the committee felt that Barry should come back into the first team in order to have at least one batsman with a bit of confidence in his form. But they then had to decide who to leave out to make way for him. The choice lay between Jessica and Carl Thomas. Jessica didn't bowl, but fielded well. Carl wasn't particularly good in the field, but could bowl at medium pace if needed.

Doc now made two crucial points. If the Australian was any good with his leg-spin bowling, there would be less likelihood of having to call on Carl to bowl. And secondly, with another spinner in the team, it was essential that the fielding and catching was as good as they could get. This tipped the scales in Jessica's favour. She kept her place in the team, but only just. Saturday's match would be a crucial one for her.

The meeting was being brought to an end when a knock came on the door. It was Jessica, who had been serving behind the bar. It must be something important because she knew full well that no-one was to interrupt a committee meeting without a very good reason indeed.

She did have a good reason. The Australian had just turned up. He was at the bar and wanted to speak to someone in authority at the club. Clive and T.G. immediately went out to meet him.

The Australian–Gary Hudson by name–was shorter than Clive had imagined. Though not fat, he was on the chunky side. He had a mop of curly fair hair and, even though he hadn't left an Australian summer, his tan was still enough to beat most people who had been sunning themselves in Blackpool for a week at the height of our summer. The only other features that were immediately noticeable about him were a stubby nose and a neatly-trimmed moustache.

After welcoming him and doing the introductions Clive told him, "We weren't expecting you till tomorrow. You should have phoned. I'd have come to meet you in Swansea."

"I like to give surprises," said Gary.

"I thought you were staying with friends in London tonight."

"I was supposed to be. But when I got round to their house there was nobody in. Their neighbours said they'd be away for another few days at least." He shook his head. "I don't understand it. They must have got the dates mixed up. Typical of you Poms."

Clive smiled, then asked, "Would you like a drink?"

"A stupid question to ask an Aussie. I'll have a lager."

"And I'll have a whisky." T.G. wasn't going to miss out on this.

Clive went to fetch the drinks and T.G. took the newcomer to a nearby table. As Jessica was serving Clive, she told him, "I hope he's as quick on the field as he is off it. He's already made a pass at me and he's only been here two minutes."

Clive raised his eyebrows. "Romance in the air perhaps?"

Jessica shook her head firmly. "Not my type. Too pushy."

"How can you say that, Jess. You've only just met him."

"Female intuition, call it what you will, but take my word for it, Clive, we're going to have problems with that one."

Clive dismissed Jessica's comments at the time, but her words kept coming back to him time and again throughout the rest of the season as problem after problem arose in relation to Marwen's newest recruit. He phoned Pat to tell her their guest had arrived. She said she'd have a meal ready for them by the time they got back. Clive told her he expected to be back by half past ten.

But he had reckoned without one Gary Hudson. By half past ten the Australian had drunk eight pints of lager. Or, as he put it, *only* eight pints. He wanted at least another two before leaving.

"But Pat's cooked us a meal," Clive said. "It'll be ready by now."

"She won't mind waiting, will she, Clive? I mean, it's my first night here and I'm getting to know everybody."

"One more pint then," sighed Clive.

"No way. I said at least two. If you want to go, go. I'll come along later."

At that moment Clive looked in the direction of the bar and saw Jessica. She just held out her hands, palms upwards, as much as to say, "What did I tell you?"

They stayed until half past eleven. The clubhouse usually closed at eleven but, as Gary told them, this was a special occasion, a welcoming evening. By the time Clive and Gary reached the house, Pat was asleep in the chair. Clive woke her up and introduced her to Gary, who told her, "Sorry we're late. It's all my fault. Clive wanted to come earlier, but I said you wouldn't mind, this being my first night here. You don't mind, do you, Pat?"

What could she say? She smiled, fetched the food, sat up with them for a few minutes, then excused herself and went to bed. After closing the bedroom door, she grabbed one of the pillows from the bed and proceeded to pummel it as hard as she could. Having vented her anger on the defenceless pillow, she got ready for bed. By the time Clive came up, she was fast asleep.

* * *

Clive left for work the following morning at half past eight and there was no sign of the Australian. Pat said she'd leave him sleep on as he was no doubt tired after the long journey and the late drinking. Well, after the long journey anyway.

By eleven o' clock he still hadn't surfaced, so Pat decided to take him a cup of tea. She tapped on the door and went in to find Gary sitting on the bed smoking a cigarette. Clive had warned her that Gary smoked, so she wasn't unprepared for the sight which greeted her. Pat was avidly anti-smoking, as Gary was about to find out.

"I've brought you a cup of tea," Pat told him. "And a warning. That's the last cigarette you'll smoke in this house. If you want to continue with that disgusting habit, you will do so outside from now on."

"But I'm a guest, Pat."

"Exactly, you're a guest. And this is my house. There's been no smoking in this house since we've been here, and that is not going to change now. Of course, if you're not happy with that, there are plenty of benches along the cricket field boundary and I'm sure you'd be welcome to use one of those."

"I was told I'd be given good lodgings here."

"And you have. But they're lodgings with a stringent no-smoking policy. No ifs or buts, no exceptions. Just plainly and simply and oh so definitely–no smoking. OK?"

Pat put the cup of tea on the cabinet beside the bed. She had made her point and was now in a hurry to get away from the smoke. But Gary wasn't going to give in easily. "Remember that I'm here to help out your cricket team."

"So I've been told. And you'd be in a far better condition to help them if you stopped inhaling that muck."

"My condition is no problem. Anyway, I don't need to run much on the pitch. I tend to score my runs in boundaries."

"Good for you. And I'll look forward to seeing that. Unless of course you'll be restricted by the stiffness."

"I haven't got any stiffness."

"You will after sleeping on one of those benches." Pat left before he could reply.

While finishing off the only cigarette he would ever smoke in that house, Gary thought to himself she's going to be a challenge. He smiled. But there was no smile on Pat's face as she made her way down the stairs. She thought to herself, he's going to be trouble.

* * *

The same conclusion would be drawn by a number of people in the village in the next few days. The first bone of contention was sex. It seemed as if Gary's prime aim was to provide a stud service for any unsatisfied women, or indeed any women, in the area. Of course these women didn't yet know of him or the new service he was providing, so he would need to rectify this. And he did so with relish. He set about accosting any women that he met, certain that he would soon strike lucky. The constant rebuttals he received did nothing to dampen his ardour. They served only to make him more determined than before. The women here were obviously completely unaware that they needed him. This he would soon put to rights.

No woman was safe from him. Young or middle-aged, married or single, attractive or plain, it didn't matter. To his mind, if she was female she was fair game. It was only the good nature of the villagers that prevented the newcomer from partaking of hospital food for the next few days. Complaints were numerous and there was talk of getting the law involved, so Clive soon had to have a word with Gary about this. He told him that if he wanted to be accepted by the village he'd have to change his ways. He should adopt a lower profile.

Gary assured Clive that he saw his point and would indeed adopt a lower profile. To Clive this meant that the problem was settled; to Gary this meant waiting until next week before taking up the reins again.

Not that the postponement of this particular problem prevented Gary from antagonising people. He seemed to have a natural flair for rubbing people up the wrong way. By the time he'd been in Marwen a week, Gary had made more enemies than friends. Mind you, if he'd made just one enemy that statement would still be true.

Jessica and Bob were two of the many who didn't take to the man from Down Under. Jessica's initial feelings about him were confirmed when he came to her father's shop on the Thursday to buy cigarettes. She had been having a cup of tea in the back room and came through to the shop to find Gary talking to her father.

Since his arrival in Marwen, Gary had heard from various people that Jessica was playing for the cricket team. Of course, he had known from the outset that they were pulling his leg and he had no intention of rising to the bait. It was quite an elaborate leg-pull too. They had even gone so far as to include her name on the team sheet for Saturday's game. But he wasn't falling for it. Even now, with T.G. describing Jessica's exploits in her early games, he wasn't fooled. He wasn't the dumb colonial they took him for.

When Jessica came in, he told her, "This is quite a wheeze you lot have got going here. I'm impressed. I didn't think you'd all be able to keep it up for so long."

Jessica was looking very serious. "This is no wheeze, Gary. It's true."

Gary chuckled knowingly and that annoyed Jessica. "I've been in the team for weeks now," she said. "Everybody knows that." He nodded and smiled and that infuriated her even more. "You can see the scorebook if you like. We've got it in the back here. We couldn't doctor that, could we. Not even for an impressive . . . wheeze."

She didn't wait for a reply; she went to the back room to fetch the scorebook she had been studying while drinking her tea. Gary now frowned. Could it be that this wasn't a leg-pull after all? Could it be that everyone had been telling the truth all along? Could it be that Jessica really did play for the team? No. Impossible. Wasn't it?

Jessica returned with the book and proudly showed him the pages covering the last few games, with her name included each time. Gary checked to see that this was indeed the club's official scorebook, then exclaimed, "Bloody hell!"

"Now do you believe us?" Jessica asked.

"This is ridiculous. I've come all this way to play cricket and find out that it's a women's team."

Jessica replied emphatically. "It is not a women's team. It's a cricket team with one woman playing in it."

"As I said, ridiculous."

"What's ridiculous about it?"

"Look, I understand that some women like to play cricket. And that's fine. There are plenty of women's teams for them to play in. But not men's teams. Men's teams are for men."

"There's no such thing as men's teams. There are cricket teams. And for a cricket team you pick the best eleven players available, whatever sex they are. Just because your Australian women may not be good enough, that doesn't mean that British women aren't."

Gary looked at Jessica for a moment, then nodded. "I suppose you're right. You've had plenty of women in the England team over the years."

T.G. had kept quiet throughout this exchange. His daughter was well capable of standing up for herself in this kind of discussion. He knew that from experience. She had stood up to him often enough. But now he could sense that she was losing her temper, so he stepped in. "There's no point talking about it any more now. You'll see her playing on Saturday, Gary. You'll see for yourself how good she is at cricket."

"Yeah, I guess so. Just as long as she doesn't drop any catches off my bowling." By now the Australian wasn't smiling. Neither was Jessica as she returned to the back room, slamming the door behind her.

* * *

Bob's first contact with Marwen's new player came later the same day when he called round at the Walters' house. Pat answered the door and was pleasantly surprised to see him.

"I thought I'd better come round and meet my replacement," he told her. "I've heard a lot about him."

"I'm sure you have," Pat said. She wondered whether anyone in the village hadn't heard of him—and he had been there only three days. She led the way into the living room, where Clive and Gary were drinking coffee. After the introductions had been made, Pat went to make a cup of coffee for Bob.

"So you're the one who broke his arm fielding," Gary said as Bob sat down.

"Yes, unfortunately," Bob replied.

"I wouldn't call it unfortunate. I'd call it bloody careless. How the hell can you break your arm fielding?"

Bob thought Gary was joking, so he just laughed. "It's an art," he said.

"I'm glad you think it's funny, mate, cos I don't. Not when we've got to have a woman in the team. All because of your bloody arm."

"Hang on now, Gary," Clive said, putting down his cup. "For one thing, Bob's accident was just that—an accident. He couldn't help it, it just happened. And for another thing, Jessica isn't in the team to make up the numbers. She's in on merit."

"Superwoman is she?"

This time Bob answered. "No, not Superwoman, just a good cricketer."

Gary sneered, "She can't be a good cricketer. She's a woman. And a woman's place is a bedroom or a kitchen, not a cricket field."

His timing was meticulous. He said that just as Pat was coming in with Bob's coffee. She turned on her new lodger immediately. "Tell me, Gary. Are all Australians like you? Or are there any enlightened people down there."

"I just think—and I bet most men think the same—that women should stick to what they can do best."

"How very progressive of you! I expect you object to women having the vote as well."

"Don't be ridiculous, Pat. I'm just saying..."

"Saying too much from where I'm standing. But perhaps that's the way Neanderthals are."

Clive intervened. "Pat!" He had to stop this before it got out of hand. He knew his wife didn't like their guest and he knew he was going to have his work cut out trying to keep the peace over the next few weeks. With Gary's antagonistic approach and Pat's inability to hide her feelings for long, a flare-up was highly likely at some point. Highly likely? It was downright inevitable. But he wanted to put it off for as long as possible. "Let's change the subject, shall we?"

The four of them talked about various things, from Welsh singing to Australian beaches, but the atmosphere was very strained. Clive could feel it, so could Bob.

Gary, on the other hand, saw nothing out of place. He thought that a good argument was a pleasant way to pass the time and he had enjoyed the one with Pat earlier. It was a pity that Clive had stopped it. Still, there'll be other chances.

After half an hour Bob got up to leave. He said he was sorry he had to go so soon, but he had arranged to take Carol out for a drink. Actually, he wasn't sorry, nor had he arranged to take Carol out. But he would remedy that very quickly. He needed a pint after all this.

"Will you be coming to the game on Saturday?" Clive asked.

"Of course," Bob replied. "I want to see how good my replacement is."

"You come and watch, Bob," said Gary. "You can then see how a good cricketer plays."

"That's what I like about you Aussies," said Bob. "Always so modest."

Gary sensed the possibility of another argument and was about to make a comment, but Bob excused himself and left before he had a chance.

Clive let Pat show Bob out. He didn't want to leave Pat and Gary on their own so soon after their earlier argument. Pat was glad to get out of the room. She wouldn't have minded getting out of the house, as she told Bob at the front door. Bob knew how she felt. He was glad he was going.

* * *

It seemed that Gary Hudson found great difficulty making friends. He seemed intent on provoking everyone he met. And he saw nothing wrong in it. But if he was going to be an asset to the cricket club on the playing side, then this was something the rest of the team, and the villagers in general, would have to put up with.

His first match was at home to Cernig. Marwen had lost heavily in Cernig in the first match of the season and Cernig were at present second in the table, so the Marwen players had little reason to feel confident. All except one, that is. The one with the markedly different accent was brimming with confidence.

Shortly before two Pete Richards and Ian Cowling walked to the wicket, Clive having won the toss and deciding to bat. The opening pair set about their task quietly and at 28 for no wicket after ten overs Marwen's position looked quite satisfactory. But five overs later the score was 31 for 3 with both opening batsmen and Steve Williams dismissed by the same bowler. Gary went in at No. 4 at the end of one over, Steve scored a single off the last ball of the next over and then was bowled by the first ball of the following over. So when Barry Roberts came in the two batsmen at the wicket had yet to face a delivery.

Both faced a number of deliveries during the next forty minutes as they set about stopping the rot which appeared to be setting in again. Gary looked impressive and displayed quite an array of strokes. By the time the 50 partnership came up, his personal tally was 29.

Barry was also looking well set. His century for the second team the previous week had done him a power of good and he was playing with far more confidence than he had shown in his previous first-team games this season. He appeared very comfortable at the crease, regardless of the bowling changes which Cernig effected to try to separate the batsmen.

T.G. remarked to Clive as they sat together watching the game, "I haven't seen Barry so relaxed in a long time. It wouldn't surprise me if he got another century today. There's no reason why he shouldn't."

No reason at all. Well, perhaps one–the person batting at the other end. Gary didn't seem to have a flaw in his stroke play, but it soon became evident that there was a great flaw in his running between the wickets. There had been one or two slight mix-ups early on in the partnership, though that was put down to the fact that they hadn't batted together before. But there was nothing slight about the mix-up when the score was 85. Barry played the ball wide of cover point and called for a single. There was a single there if Gary went immediately. But he didn't. He stayed his ground and yelled at Barry to go back. By now Barry was well down the wicket. He stopped, turned and ran back. But it was too late. He was run out.

Barry glared at his batting partner–or, rather, his ex-batting partner. The latter simply shrugged his shoulders.

Barry had scored 23 when he was run out. Kevin was next in and he hadn't scored anything when the Australian caused him to be run out. With the score on 87, Gary played the ball in front of him and, as there were no close fielders, he called for a single and ran. Kevin responded, but not as quickly as the bowler, who ran to the ball and threw it at the stumps, hitting them before Kevin reached safety.

Kevin turned to the other batsman. "You idiot!" he said. "What the hell are you playing at?"

The Australian shrugged his shoulders again.

The next batsman in was Clive. As the incoming batsman passed the outgoing batsman, Kevin told his skipper, "You'd better put roller blades on if you intend staying out there with that kangaroo."

Clive didn't smile. The situation wasn't amusing. He played out the rest of the over, then went to have a word with Gary, impressing on him the need for greater caution in running between the wickets. Gary heeded the word of caution, yet there were still some minor scares as he and Clive tried to halt another Marwen slide. Clive played sensibly and his calming influence undoubtedly had an effect on Gary's play.

They took the score to 108 when Gary, on 42, received a long-hop from the off-spinner who was now bowling. The batsman tried to give it the treatment it deserved, but was caught on the boundary. All the Cernig players applauded the catch. As did two players in the Marwen changing room.

As Gary was leaving the field, Jessica was going to the wicket. As they passed each other, the Australian said, "I see we're down to the tail then."

Jessica said nothing, but inside she was seething. As if she didn't have enough problems. She was playing for her place today. The last thing she wanted was a comment like that. She tried to put it out of her mind and concentrate on her batting. But it wasn't her day. With her score on 1 she received what was probably the best delivery of the innings, a good length ball which cut away off the seam. It would have tested the best of batsmen. Jessica was caught behind, Marwen were 111 for 7.

The tail didn't wag much and Marwen were all out for 123. They had three batting points, but everyone knew it could have been more if it hadn't been for the run-outs.

This had already been pointed out to Gary when he had left the field. Barry and Kevin left him in no doubt as to their opinion. Yet he would accept none of the blame. "I don't know what you're whining about. There was never a run with the first one. And as for the second, if you can't run quickly enough, old boy, you should take up bowls or dominoes." Barry had to hold Kevin back at that point. The Australian went on. "Anyway, look at the score. Where would you lot be if I hadn't been playing?"

Barry felt like saying, "I'd probably still be out there," but he wanted to calm things down before anything serious happened, so he said nothing. He knew of Kevin's temper, so the best thing to do was take him out and give him a chance to cool down.

* * *

After tea Clive had a word with the team in the changing room. He was aware of the rumblings of dissatisfaction among some of the players and he wanted to put an end to them immediately. "What's happened has happened," he said. "What's important now is for us to go out there as one team–united. I don't want to hear any snide comments. We've got to play with each other and for each other. All we need to be concerned with is getting them out for less than 123. Now come on."

He gave no-one else the opportunity to speak. This wasn't a matter for discussion. He led the team out.

Cernig knew that a win today might take them to the top of the table. They had already put themselves in a strong position and they were determined not to miss out now.

It was widely recognised that Cernig's opening batsmen were the best in the Division and they showed why as they played the Marwen opening attack with ease, with contempt even.

With the score at 41, Clive decided to switch to spin. He

brought John Price on as the first change and three overs later brought Gary on at the other end to bowl his leg-spin. There were very few leg-spinners in the League, so it was likely that Gary, if he was any good, could well pose problems for a number of batsmen during the remainder of the season. But was he any good? It didn't seem so in his first few overs as the Cernig batsmen seemed to hit him all over the place. Three overs cost 24 runs.

Everybody was expecting Clive to take him off, but the captain decided to give him one more over. In that fourth over Gary seemed to settle into a better rhythm and the batsmen found it more difficult to get him away. Only one run came off the over, so Clive decided to keep him on.

John, on the other hand, had been bowling tidily throughout and with the score on 72 he could have taken the first wicket. It was the first mistake either of the batsmen had made. The ball was driven towards mid-off. Jessica was fielding there, but as the ball was coming towards her, she heard a voice yell, "Catch it, Jessie baby." For one instant her concentration was broken. That was enough to cause the catch to go down.

She was furious with herself. She was even more furious when she heard the same voice, with an Australian accent, say, "That's what comes of having a woman in the team."

This definitely wasn't Jessica's day. In the next over the ball was skied and she was the fielder underneath it, waiting for it to come down. Her mind was racing as she waited. She knew who the bowler was. She knew she had to catch it. She daren't drop it. She... Oh no! The ball was on the ground. She wasn't sure how it had got there, but there it was. How on earth could she have done it? It wasn't a difficult catch. She had held ones that were far more difficult. It was just all that waiting, all that thinking.

"Oh, bloody hell!" No need to say who was speaking. "Clive, can you put this woman out of the way somewhere. Behind the bar preferably."

Clive, at mid-on, told him, "Leave it, Gary. I've said there are to be no comments and I mean it. Jess stays where she is."

Clive knew what it would do to Jessica's confidence if he

moved her now. But it was too late. Her confidence had totally evaporated anyway. She couldn't wait for the game to end. Perhaps she wasn't cut out to be a cricketer after all. Perhaps Gary was right. Perhaps she should be left behind the bar. She wanted to run off and have a good cry somewhere. But she couldn't. She had to stay here and play out her last game for the club.

Considering the start Cernig had made, Marwen did very well after the dropped catches. The first wicket went down with the score at 94 and by the time Cernig reached their target they had lost five wickets. John took two wickets, Gary three. Had the target been 40 or 50 more, it could have been an interesting finish. But it wasn't and another game was lost.

A few of the Marwen players tried to console Jessica as they left the field. But she was inconsolable. After changing she went to serve behind the bar and stayed there until the club closed, saying very little to anyone. She was in no mood for talking.

T.G. knew this and kept quiet as they walked home together. They spoke very little in the house afterwards. Best to say nothing, leave it until tomorrow. Plenty of time to talk then.

* * *

The taking of those five Cernig wickets in a relatively short space of time seemed to indicate a possible avenue of escape from Marwen's impending relegation. Once Gary had found his rhythm with the ball, he and John had caused no end of difficulties for the batsmen. If they could continue in this vein in the coming matches, there might still be hope.

But there were two other factors to take into account that tended to diminish this hope. One was the brittle nature of the Marwen batting. Having two bowlers capable of causing problems for the opposition was of little use unless their own batsmen gave them a tidy total to bowl at.

The second factor, of course, was the dropping of catches. Spin bowlers in particular depend on fielders talking catches when the opportunities come. The way Marwen's players were dropping catches this season, this would be the last team on earth a spin bowler would want to join. The fielding would have to improve and the catches would have to be taken. But they had been saying that for a long time and still nothing had changed. Even the previously dependable Jessica had started putting chances down.

* * *

As expected, Jessica was dropped for the next game, away to Plasmawr, and Carl Thomas was recalled.

Plasmawr batted first and although Steve Williams took an early wicket, they looked set for a big score at 53 for 1 after ten overs. Clive then opted for a double bowling change, bringing on both his spinners. They made an immediate impact, slowing down the run rate, and then the wickets started to fall. In a dramatic collapse Plasmawr went from 59 for 1 to 85 all out. Gary took five wickets, John three and there was one run-out.

It was amazing. Ian told Clive as they left the field, "I thought we were the only ones who could manage collapses like that." What made it more amazing was that four catches had been taken out of a possible five. The only person to drop a catch was Clive himself.

So here at last was an ideal opportunity to win a match and pick up some much-needed points. But Clive warned his players not to be complacent. "This isn't the best of pitches," he told them, "so don't take any chances. Just take the runs as they come. What I want out there today is steady batting... and no collapse."

Clive made only slight changes to the batting order, putting Carl in at No. 3 and moving Steve down to No. 8. Steve wasn't having the happiest of times with the bat and Clive felt it advisable to let him go in later for a while.

The changes didn't prevent an early collapse. After eight overs, the score was 25 for 3. The target of 86 to win now looked a lot more difficult.

Gary and Barry were at the wicket and they again steadied the innings, as they had done the previous week. There was one difference this week—Barry was much more wary of running between the wickets and he took not the slightest chance of running any quick singles. The 50 was reached without further loss and again Marwen seemed set for victory.

Unfortunately, this was not to be. The clouds that had started to gather at the start of the innings now thickened and by the time the score had reached 58 for 3, the rain was coming down steadily.

Gary wasn't bothered, he wanted to carry on regardless. The Plasmawr players, of course, wanted to come off, intimating to the umpires that these were impossible conditions for the bowlers. The umpires brought the players off, and off they stayed. The rain kept falling steadily. It didn't get any worse, but neither did it lessen at all.

Gary argued with the Plasmawr players that they should let the game reach its conclusion, but they didn't want to know. He couldn't understand why the rest of his team said nothing. Shouldn't they be complaining as well? As Clive then told him, if he had been at the Ramley game a few weeks earlier he'd know now there was no point complaining.

So the match was drawn and Marwen were still firmly rooted to the bottom of the table. But they had come close this time. Very close. Perhaps in the coming matches they would go all the way.

The Australian was proving a valuable acquisition. He was an absolute pain off the field, but he was providing them with a chance of avoiding the drop; and as long as he did that, he would be a pain they'd be prepared to suffer.

Chapter 8

LOVE IS A MANY SPLINTERED THING

The mood in the next committee meeting was more optimistic than it had been for some time. Although the team hadn't picked up the twelve points for a win at Plasmawr, they had secured a moral victory. And any sort of victory was welcome under the present circumstances.

The committee members were happy with the way the newcomer was playing, apart from some reservations regarding his ability to judge quick singles and they were over the proverbial moon at the prospect of having a weapon in the form of their spin bowlers which could yet haul them out of trouble.

T.G. said, "If our opening bowlers had half the success of the spinners, we'd be well on our way."

"You can't blame the lads," Clive said. "Andy and Steve are still very young, remember."

"I know, I know. But it's annoying to give so many runs away before we stand a real chance of breaking through the batting."

Doc now put forward a suggestion that was to raise eyebrows all around the local cricket scene during the coming weeks. "Why do we have to wait before bringing the spinners on? Why not open the bowling with them?"

"You can't open with two spinners," the chairman said.

"Why not?" asked Doc.

There was no reason why not. Clive was in favour of the idea.

He himself had been thinking of bringing on the spinners after only six or seven overs in the next game, but he might just as well put them on at the start.

Doc furthered his argument. "If we open with our spinners we'll have our main wicket-takers on from the start and it'll unnerve the opposition batsmen before a ball is bowled. They won't know what's going on."

Everyone agreed it was worth a try, but Doc sounded a note of caution. "Of course, it makes it even more important that our fielders hold their catches. If they're going to keep dropping the catches that come, there's no point trying this."

Clive came to his team's defence. "Things are improving there, Doc. We held nearly all our chances on Saturday."

"All except one," said Arthur, looking directly at Clive. "And we all know who dropped that."

Clive blushed. Even more so when the others laughed.

Glyn James reported that the Seconds had lost on Saturday and he gave a brief account of the game to let the others know how the various players had performed.

T.G. already knew as Jessica had been playing in the game and had told him about it. After much persuading from her father, Jessica had agreed to try a couple of games in the second team before making a final decision as regards giving up playing cricket. This was a far cry from T.G.'s attitude earlier in the season when he didn't want her playing in any team. He was now more in favour of her playing than she was. As he told her, "You've proved to me you can play, now prove it to yourself."

Unfortunately, she didn't do that in her first game for the Seconds. She again failed with the bat, scoring only two runs. When T.G. arrived back from the first team's match at Plasmawr, she told him that she would try just once more and if she failed again, that was it.

* * *

This was one of the matters T.G. and Clive discussed in the bar after the committee meeting. Clive said he was sorry things had turned out as they had. He felt sure that Jessica could do well, but if she really wanted to give up, then she should be allowed to do so. Perhaps after a while her old enthusiasm would return.

T.G. then turned the conversation to another problem that had been worrying him. Though this particular problem didn't affect him directly. "Now about Kevin," he said.

"What about Kevin?" Clive asked.

"You know," the chairman replied.

"If I knew, I wouldn't have asked."

"His ... er ... involvement with that woman. You must have heard about it. It's all around the village."

"No, I haven't heard about it and I don't think I want to hear about it. I don't see that Kevin's private life is any of our business."

"It'll become our business when we play Ramley again."

Clive looked blankly at T.G. He was still in total ignorance as to why this conversation was taking place. They had never before discussed any of Kevin's numerous relationships. T.G.'s next sentence enlightened Clive. "The woman he's having an affair with is Stuart Wilkins's wife."

Clive couldn't believe his ears. "Catherine? You're joking."

"Do I look as if I'm joking? Now what are you going to do about it?"

"Nothing," said Clive emphatically. "If what you say is true, it's still none of our business. When we play Ramley, we concern ourselves with the cricket. And only the cricket. Any other games that are going on are the concern of the people playing those games. We keep our noses out, T.G. Right?"

"But ... "

"Right?"

T.G. was reluctant to let the matter drop but was soon mollified by Clive's offer of another drink. As Clive went to fetch the drinks he reflected on the news T.G. had given him. There could indeed be problems as a result of this.

When he got home he spoke to Pat about it. She had been out with Jessica for the evening, the first time they had managed to get out together for a couple of weeks, and had heard the news from her. Apparently the affair had started soon after the Ramley game.

Clive remembered sensing after that game that all was not well between Stuart Wilkins and his wife. But he hadn't expected anything like this. Should he say anything to Kevin in view of all the talk that apparently was doing the rounds in the village? Or should he keep out of it completely? Clive didn't know what was best. He slept very uneasily that night.

* * *

On his way home from work on the Wednesday Clive called to see Bob to give him a form regarding the insurance claim following his accident. While he was there, he brought up the matter of Kevin's affair, knowing Bob to be Kevin's best friend. Bob said he had tried to reason with Kevin about it but had been told in no uncertain terms to keep out of it.

"Should I have a word with him?" Clive asked.

Bob shook his head. "No point. He wouldn't listen. Anyway, he's a big boy now, old enough to look after himself. He's got himself into this and he's going to have to get himself out of it."

The matter was left there. Clive didn't say so, but he had decided that if an opportunity arose he would have a word with Kevin.

The opportunity arose the following evening. Gary had gone to Swansea for the evening and Pat had gone to see her mother, so Clive decided to go down to the clubhouse for a quiet drink. Bob and Kevin were there and Clive, having bought a pint of lager, joined them.

When Doc came in a few minutes later, Bob went over to talk to him about the insurance claim. This left Clive and Kevin together and it wasn't long before Clive brought up the matter that had been troubling him. "You know people are talking about you and the Wilkins woman."

"Her name is Catherine, as you know very well," Kevin replied sternly. "And as for village gossip, it doesn't bother me. It's none of their business. And it's none of yours either."

"It'll probably be my business when we go to play Ramley.

A Good Catch

How do you think they're going to look at it?"

"If that's what you're worried about, I'll drop out for that game. Or if you like, I'll drop out of the side completely."

"There's no need for that, Kev. And it's not really the Ramley game that worries me. It's you and what you're getting yourself into."

Kevin stopped him from going any further. "If you're going to give me the 'She's a married woman' speech, don't bother. I've already had that from Bob. And I told him what he could do with it."

Clive thought it best to say nothing more now, as Kevin was obviously beginning to get worked up. Best to give him a chance to cool down.

Kevin drank some of his lager, then put the glass down and looked at it. "Anyway," he said, "she's left her husband now. She's staying with a friend in Temway." He fiddled with the glass. "I wanted her to move in with me." (He had the house to himself at present as the two who had been sharing with him had found work in London for the next few months.) "But she wants time to sort herself out." He looked up at Clive. "And that's all it is . . . a matter of time."

Clive raised his eyebrows. "Frankly, Kev, I'm amazed that the two of you could consider living together. From what I've seen of Catherine and from what I know of you, you've got next to nothing in common." He shrugged his shoulders. "OK, there's the physical side. But there's got to be more, hasn't there. You're not going to be in bed all the time."

Kevin slammed his fist on the table. "Listen, Clive, keep your bloody nose out of my business or . . . or I'll make it my business to give you a bloody nose. Right?" He then stormed out.

Clive shook his head. He had just touched a very raw nerve. Kevin had known Catherine for only a short time, but was becoming increasingly aware that their interests did indeed differ greatly. He himself had wondered how much of a problem that would be, but he didn't want other people pointing out the problem to him.

Anyway, there was no problem really, He could get to like the things she liked. In fact, on Friday evening they were going to a concert in Cardiff to listen to some orchestra or other. He wasn't particularly keen on classical music, but Catherine liked it and she had managed to get tickets, which apparently was some achievement given the demand for them. So Kevin would put up with it, he might even enjoy it. The important thing was that she had a weekend off and they were going to spend it together.

* * *

On Saturday morning Kevin stayed in bed late. He was tired after the trip to Cardiff the previous evening. And what a bore that was. How could people sit for hours listening to that? Clive's words came back to him, but he quickly dismissed them.

When he eventually got up, he found that Catherine had been tidying the house. He'd never seen the place so clean. The only problem was he didn't know where anything was. It took him some time to find all his cricket gear ready for today's match. Still, he shouldn't grumble. She'd done a good job on the house.

He left for the ground at ten to two. Catherine was going to spend the afternoon with friends and in the evening they would pick up Kevin and the four of them would go out for a meal.

* * *

Marwen's opponents were Penford, whose captain won the toss and put Marwen in to bat. He knew how brittle their batting was and wanted to have an easy target for his own batsmen. What he didn't foresee was Marwen's best batting performance of the season. Ian and Pete put on 60 runs for the first wicket and when Ian was caught behind for 34, Gary went in, having been moved up to No. 3.

The Australian didn't take long to get into his stride but soon lost his first partner. Pete was run out, but this time no-one could blame Gary. Gary played the ball past cover point and the fielder chased it to the boundary. Pete called for a third run when Gary

A Good Catch

would have settled for two and a good throw left Pete a metre out of his crease.

Barry was next in and he and Gary, as in previous matches, set about the bowling in an accomplished manner. But this was not to be one of Gary's best days with the bat and he was bowled for 25, which to him was a disappointing failure.

Barry kept going, ably supported by Carl and when Barry was caught on the long-on boundary for 41, the score had reached 145 for 4 with just under nine overs to go. Three deliveries later the score was 145 for 5. Kevin was l.b.w. for a duck.

But that was the last wicket to fall. Clive was next in and he and Carl saw Marwen through to a total of 186 for 5, with Clive 18 not out and Carl 27 not out. It had been a good all-round performance—with one exception.

After tea the Penford opening batsmen, indeed the whole Penford team, were surprised to see Gary open the bowling. They were even more surprised when they saw John Price coming on at the other end. What were Marwen playing at? The answer soon became evident. Both the opening batsmen were back in the changing room before the score had reached double figures.

After that the wickets kept falling steadily and Penford were all out for 53. The only blemish as far as Marwen were concerned was Kevin's performance. He dropped two catches and misfielded when there was a very good chance of a run-out.

John took four wickets and Gary six, including one spectacular caught-and-bowled. The batsman had played forward and the ball didn't rise very much, but Gary dived forward and got his right hand beneath it before it touched the ground. As he got up, he turned to Kevin and said, "Now do you know what to do?"

Kevin didn't get worked up about the comment. It was obvious that his mind was elsewhere. It was equally obvious where it was.

As the players came off at the end of the game, Clive took Kevin aside. "Listen, Kev, in future when you play for us I don't just want your body out there, I want your mind as well. You told me before it was none of my business, but when you play the way you did today that makes it my business. Get yourself sorted out.

And quickly. Or you're going to find yourself out on your arse as far as this team is concerned."

Clive didn't wait for a reply. He went to join the others in the changing room. The mood in there, needless to say, was euphoric.

Kevin was very subdued as he changed. He didn't join in any of the banter, nor did he bother replying when Gary taunted him about his performance. "With ten more like you out there, Kev, we wouldn't have stood a chance. I hope you perform better tonight."

"That's enough!" said Clive firmly. He'd had his say with Kevin. He didn't want anyone else chipping in, particularly Gary.

Kevin changed quickly and went straight to the car park. He hurried towards Catherine's Mini Cooper, in which she was waiting with her two friends, Dave and Barbara. Dave was an accountant and Barbara a lecturer in one of the local colleges. She and Catherine had been friends ever since going to school together.

Kevin didn't have an enjoyable time at all that evening. He didn't like Catherine's friends and made little attempt to hide his feelings. During the meal they had gone on and on about their visits to this country and that. They went abroad four or five times a year. "Oh that we could afford the time and money to go more often," Barbara said. Kevin felt like throwing up.

Then for what seemed like an eternity to Kevin, they went through their likes and dislikes of each country. When eventually they did pause, Kevin took his chance. "Personally, I don't see the point of going abroad all the time," he said. "We've got plenty of terrific places in this country. You can keep your Spains and your Frances, give me Bournemouth every time." Kevin enjoyed that little speech, particularly as he'd never been to Bournemouth in his life.

They all went back to Kevin's house for coffee, on Catherine's invitation, but Dave and Barbara didn't stay long. They could feel Kevin's animosity towards them. They would have had to be either stupid or dead not to have felt it.

Catherine offered to drive them home, but they insisted on

ordering a taxi. After they had gone, Catherine left Kevin in no doubt that she was absolutely disgusted with the way he had treated her friends. Kevin shrugged his shoulders and sniggered, "They're snobs. And I can't stand snobs."

"They're not snobs," Catherine replied. "They're very intelligent people and have done very well for themselves. Just because they show up your deficiencies, there's no need to insult them."

That hurt. But Catherine didn't let up. "I'd spoken so highly of you all afternoon and they were really looking forward to meeting you. Then you turn up and behave like an absolute imbecile. I was so ashamed." That comment struck home too. "If it wasn't so late and I wasn't so tired I'd go now. As it is, I'll leave first thing in the morning. I assume you'll let me have your bed and you'll find somewhere else to sleep." She got up and left the room without another word.

Kevin sat quietly on the rug, thinking over what had happened. Clive's words came back to him again; "You've got next to nothing in common." It was becoming increasingly obvious that they did indeed have very little in common. But then again, don't they say that opposites attract? Perhaps that was the case with him and Catherine. Or was it?

He liked her, but didn't like her friends. Well, the two he'd met tonight anyway. But not all her friends would be like that. Would they? And what about his friends? He didn't know what she'd think of them. After what she'd just said, he didn't really know what she thought of him. Deficiencies? Ashamed?

So, where would they go from here? Perhaps nowhere after this. Perhaps it was after all nothing more than a wild fling. Yet they had talked of a future together. But what sort of a future? Before reaching any sort of conclusion Kevin fell asleep.

* * *

He was still on the rug when Catherine woke him in the morning. She had brought him a cup of tea. She knelt beside him and kissed his cheek. "Morning, handsome." Giving him the tea, she said, "A little peace offering. I'm sorry about last night."

Kevin gradually came to his senses. Bringing himself up to lean on one elbow, he said sleepily, "That's OK, but..."

She put her hand over his mouth. "No buts. Remember it's worth having rows sometimes in order to have the making up afterwards."

She lay down by his side. Last night's argument was soon forgotten in the passion that followed. The cup of tea was also forgotten. Kevin knocked it over as he got up later.

* * *

They didn't see each other for a couple of days, but on Wednesday Catherine phoned to say she had bought two tickets to see a performance of "King Lear" the following evening in Swansea. Kevin agreed to go but wasn't looking forward to it. A concert and King Lear in one week. This was more culture than any normal man should be expected to take.

It was on the way from the theatre that Kevin first told Catherine of his doubts concerning their relationship. He had finalised his decision while watching the play earlier. Well, not watching exactly. After the first few minutes he'd given up trying to follow what was being said. They should have had subtitles.

"Perhaps we're too different," he said. "Nobody's fault. Just the way things are."

"Don't say that, Kev. Yes, we may have different tastes in some things, but we do suit each other. We do."

Kevin shook his head. "I'm not so sure any more. Take tonight. I mean, me going to watch Shakespeare."

Catherine was wondering why Kevin was talking like this. "It's last weekend, isn't it," she said. "I've told you I'm sorry. I didn't mean the things I said."

"It's not that, Cath. It's just... well, us. As I said, nobody's fault."

They walked and talked for some time, Catherine trying to reason with him and Kevin holding fast to a decision which he knew was right for him. By the time they reached Kevin's car

A Good Catch

Catherine had stopped trying to convince him that they did have a future together, feeling that it was best to leave him have time to think. Little was said on the journey to Temway, but as she got out of the car she told him, "Think over what I said earlier, Kev. And think carefully. I'll ring you tomorrow."

Before Kevin could reply, she shut the door and ran to the house where she was staying. Kevin drove off, feeling as if a weight had been lifted from his shoulders.

He didn't answer the phone at all when she called. Perhaps now she would accept his decision. Perhaps now she would see that this was for the best. But that wasn't being very realistic. Catherine wasn't one to give up that easily.

* * *

Kevin was back in Temway on Saturday, this time with the Marwen team. Their victory over Temway had been the only one gained in the first half of the season, so hopes were high of another win today. As expected, the committee had selected an unchanged team, but Kevin told Clive as they walked to the changing room together, "You've got one more player this week, skip. I'm back—body and mind."

"Glad to hear it, Kev," said Clive, slapping the younger man on the back.

There was an extra spectator today too. Jessica had come to watch. After another disappointing game for the Seconds the previous Saturday, when she scored 8, Jessica had decided to give up playing cricket, at least for the time being.

While waiting for Dai Davies, the Temway captain, to come out, Clive was talking to one of the umpires, whom he had known for years. His name was Fred Richards and he was one of the real characters on the local cricket scene.

"Don't take this personally," Fred told Clive, "but I hope your team manages another of its famous batting collapses today. I've got a dinner tonight and I've got to be away from here by seven."

"I don't think we'll collapse today, Fred," said Clive. "You'd better have a word with their team instead. Or cancel the dinner."

"Cancel? No way. Not at those prices."

Clive laughed. Dai now appeared and the two captains went to the wicket for the toss-up. Dai won the toss and put Marwen in to bat. There was plenty of cloud clover and he felt this would help his bowlers.

Help them it did and in no time at all Marwen were 13 for 3 with Ian (0), Pete (2) and Barry (5) back in the pavilion. Gary was still at the wicket but wasn't batting with his usual flourish. He wasn't able to as the ball was swinging so much.

He and Carl seemed to be steadying the innings, but Carl was deceived by an inswinger which took his middle stump and Marwen were 28 for 4.

Kevin was next in and he and Gary took the total past 50 before Gary was l.b.w. for 19. It was a very dubious decision because the ball had swung so much it might well have been missing leg stick. Gary looked hard at the umpire who had given him out, but Fred Richards was not to be moved. He had made his decision and that was that. He was determined that this game would be over by seven.

As Clive went to the wicket, it started to rain. He hadn't had time to take guard when the downpour came. All the players ran off, as did the umpires, though one of those was far from happy with the situation.

They were off for half an hour, then the rain stopped as suddenly as it had started. The scoreboard showed 53 for 5 as the players walked out again. Runs were just as hard to come by after play resumed and the batsmen found that their main objective was survival. None of the remaining batsmen scored many runs, but they did manage to stay at the wicket for some time to use up the overs—much to the annoyance of Fred Richards. In the end Marwen were all out for 84, with Gary and Kevin (15) the only batsmen to reach double figures.

It rained again during the tea interval and the players didn't take the field until a little after half past five. As they were walking out, Clive told Fred, "Looks as if you're going to miss the first course, Fred."

A Good Catch

"Do you want to bet?" the umpire asked, walking away.

Clive went to have a word with John Price, who was going to open the bowling from the end at which Fred was umpiring. "Anything that hits the pads, give a shout," he told the bowler without giving an explanation.

John's first over was a maiden, as was Gary's first at the other end. In John's second over the first ball was hit through the covers for four. The second ball pitched just outside off-stump, came back and hit the batsman's pad. Had the batsman not played a stroke, he would have been given out. But he had played a stroke, so he'd be alright. Or so he thought.

John appealed and the umpire raised his finger. The batsman couldn't believe it. "You've got to be joking," he said. "That pitched outside off-stick. I can't be out."

Fred replied, "It pitched in line with off-stick and you are out."

"Bloody hell," muttered the batsman. "What sort of umpire is that?"

Clive, at slip, thought to himself, "The sort that wants to be away by seven."

Fred gave three more l.b.w. decisions during the course of the innings and only one of those was beyond dispute.

Fortunately, Gary took five wickets at the other end and Fred couldn't take any of the credit for those. The batsmen found Gary almost unplayable and his final figures of 5 for 11 showed that he was indeed a bowler to be respected.

John took 4 for 28 and there was a run-out. The run-out resulted from an attempt to take a quick single. Steve, running in from mid-wicket, threw at the stumps and the ball hit them just as the batsman reached the crease. It was touch and go. But, as Fred was the umpire involved, it was go as far as the batsman was concerned.

Temway were all out for 42 at five minutes to seven. Fred followed the players from the field, grabbed his coat and left immediately. He would be in time for the first course.

It was fortunate for him that he did leave immediately. Had he stayed, there might have been more than a little unpleasantness.

After today's performance this was one umpire for whom this particular hillside would not keep a welcome.

* * *

Still, Marwen were happy. For the first time this season they had secured back-to-back wins. They might yet avoid relegation. The players were in a jubilant mood as they changed. All except Kevin. He was very pensive. It was nothing to do with the game. His batting had been better than most today and in the field he seemed to be getting back to his old self. He had taken a very difficult catch off Gary's bowling, for which even the Australian had proffered a modicum of praise.

What was troubling Kevin was that he had noticed Catherine's Mini Cooper in the car park as he left the field. She would be waiting for him. He couldn't get away quickly because he hadn't brought his own car. It was in the garage being repaired. A relatively minor job–Kevin would have it back on Monday–but a relatively major problem for Kevin because Clive had insisted on giving him a lift and, as captain, Clive would be obliged to wait for a while afterwards.

Kevin changed quietly, then went with the others to the bar. He wasn't looking forward to this.

Sure enough, Catherine was waiting and when the players came in she went over to Kevin immediately and led him away from the others. "I must talk to you," she said.

"There's nothing to talk about, "Kevin told her. "Let's just leave it. It's over. OK?"

"No, it's not OK."

"It is as far as I'm concerned. Now if you'll excuse me..."

Kevin went to move away, but Catherine caught his arm.

"Don't walk away from me when I'm talking to you," she said.

Kevin shook his arm free. "I'm going, Cath."

"I don't think so, Kevin. If you go now I'll..."

She didn't get a chance to complete her threat. Jessica had been standing nearby and had noticed what was going on. She came over, took Kevin by the arm and said, "You took your time,

Kev. Come on or we'll be late." Turning to Catherine, she added, "Excuse us, won't you. We've got to go." Then she led Kevin quickly out through the door.

Neither Kevin nor Catherine had the chance to say anything. When Catherine came to her senses, she followed them out, but by the time she got to the car park, Kevin was being driven away in Jessica's Cortina. Catherine yelled, "I'll ring you tomorrow. We need to talk."

As Jessica drove away from the ground, Kevin turned to her and asked, "Can you tell me exactly what's happening?"

Jessica smiled. "I thought you were, shall we say, having problems and that a quick exit was called for. Sorry if I was wrong. I'll turn back if you like."

"No thanks, Jess. Keep driving." Kevin sighed. "It was getting rather awkward in there. I don't know what she'd have done next."

"You will get involved with these married women."

"Only this once. Never before and, I can assure you, never again."

"We'll see." She glanced over and could see how serious he was. "You look as if you need a drink."

"Wrong. I look as if I need a lot of drinks." He turned to her. "Fancy joining me."

"Why not?"

Jessica's hopes were raised again. She was glad that Kevin's affair with Catherine Wilkins was over. Now she herself might stand a chance. Not immediately perhaps. But in time . . .

Chapter 9

DECISIONS, DECISIONS

The following afternoon Kevin was walking through the village, trying to clear his mind. Catherine had phoned a number of times during the morning and in the end he had relented and answered. He told her again that it was all over and that she should accept that, but she wouldn't listen. She insisted on talking to him in person. If he wouldn't agree to a meeting, she would come round to the house–and keep coming round until they spoke face to face. In the end he agreed to meet her in the Royal Oak in Temway on Tuesday.

As he was walking he wondered whether it was wise to meet her. But what was the alternative? Phone calls every day. Expecting her to be waiting whenever he went home. Or indeed whenever he went anywhere. No, better to meet her away from everyone and get it over with.

His thoughts were interrupted by someone calling from the opposite side of the road. It was Jessica. He crossed to speak to her.

"You were miles away then, Kev," she told him.

Kevin nodded. "Sorting a few things out in my mind."

She guessed what those few things were., so she said no more.

"Anyway, I'm glad I've bumped into you, Jess. Thanks again for your help last night. And for the sympathetic ear afterwards."

"No probs. What are friends for?"

"We'll have to go for a drink again sometime, but next time

without the agony aunt business."

She smiled. "I'll look forward to it."

Wouldn't she just. She had waited a long time to hear Kevin say that. They now went their separate ways, Kevin walking on the pavement, Jessica walking on air.

* * *

While Kevin would probably not as yet be in agreement with the arrangements Jessica was making in her mind for their future, Bob definitely wouldn't be in agreement with the arrangements Carol was making for them for the coming Saturday. As they sat in the park together on Sunday evening, Carol told Bob about these arrangements.

It would be her parents' wedding anniversary on Saturday and Carol had arranged a special celebration, booking twelve places at a restaurant in Mumbles, outside Swansea. Her two sisters, both living in Cardiff with their respective families, would go directly with their families to the restaurant. Carol and Bob would take Mr and Mrs Treharne for a run in the car, probably somewhere on the Gower peninsula, before joining the others. The whole thing was to be kept a secret from her parents.

Bob wasn't too happy. "What about the game?" he asked. "The lads are chasing three wins in a row. If they win this one, they could be off the bottom."

"So?"

"I'd like to be there to see it."

"Listen here, Robert, Saturday is very important to me and I want you to be part of it. Is Saturday's game more important to you than that?"

"Er . . . " Bob was thinking of the best way to answer.

"You mean you've got to think before answering? There shouldn't be any hesitation." Carol was on her feet now. "I'm beginning to feel you think more of that cricket team than you do of me. Every week the same. They get priority. Even after breaking your arm. Well, this week it's got to be different. Or we're finished. Do you hear, Robert Evans? Finished. You decide.

The cricket club or me."

Bob patted the bench with his left hand. "Come and sit down, babe."

"Don't babe me. I want your decision."

Bob hesitated again before answering.

"And the fact that you've got to think before answering... well, it doesn't say much for me, does it."

Bob kept calm as usual. "Now, as I see it..."

"Don't give me an analysis of the situation, Robert. Just give me your decision. Where are you going on Saturday?"

"OK, you want a decision," said Bob firmly. "At two o' clock on Saturday I'll be down the cricket club."

"Well, that's that then," said Carol and started to walk away.

Bob carried on. "But at four o' clock I'll be round your house ready to go with you and your parents to the Gower." Carol stopped and turned. Bob was smiling. "Now will you come back and sit here?"

She did.

* * *

Gary Hudson felt like a change this week. He had been going to Swansea three nights a week for the past few weeks in his continual search for 'action'. But this week he thought he would try Llanelli.

On Tuesday he went there for the first time. Pat and Clive were now well used to Gary staying out all night, so when he didn't return they thought nothing of it. "Some poor girl in Llanelli is stuck with him," Clive thought aloud. "Still, her loss is our gain."

Actually, there was no girl in Llanelli stuck with him. Gary spent the night in one of the cells in Llanelli Police Station.

He had been round a few of the pubs in the town and by ten o'clock was somewhat the worse for drink. He had spent the previous ten minutes eyeing an attractive blonde who was having a drink with her boyfriend at a nearby table. When the boyfriend went to the bar, Gary went over to the girl and sat down. "Can't you get rid of him?" he asked her.

"Why don't you try?" she asked in turn. "He's standing right behind you."

A Good Catch

Sure enough, there he was. He had seen Gary go over to the girl and had left the bar immediately. "Yeah, why don't you try?" he said.

Gary looked up at the man and it seemed to him that he was about eight foot tall. But after all he had drunk that evening Gary felt himself to be at least nine foot, so he got up and asked the man if he wanted to make an issue of it. As he lay on his back three seconds later, Gary reckoned that the man did indeed want to make an issue of it. While getting to his feet, Gary noticed an unusual pattern in the carpet. A few seconds later he was able to inspect the pattern at close quarters.

He found it more difficult to get up this time. But the landlord helped him to his feet, then helped him to the door, telling him he didn't want to see him in there again.

There was another pub just down the road. Gary went there, drank another pint of lager, then left. The place was too boring. He looked for another pub but didn't find one. Not that there wasn't one to be found. It was just that he had tripped over a loose paving stone and fallen over and, finding the pavement to his liking, had gone to sleep there.

When he woke up he was in a cell in the police station. In the morning when the police let him go, with just a warning this time, Gary thanked them for their hospitality and promised to recommend them to all his friends. Of course, they didn't know that he didn't have any friends.

So that was Llanelli. Gary wasn't very impressed. But it doesn't pay to make hasty judgements, so he'd go back again on Thursday.

* * *

The same evening that Gary was on his first hunting expedition in Llanelli, Catherine and Kevin were talking in a quiet corner of a pub some twenty miles away, the Royal Oak in Temway. Kevin came straight to the point. "I don't want to be long, Cath. So say what you have to say, then I can go."

"You didn't used to be in such a hurry to leave me," she said.

"That was then. This is now. Come on, Cath. What's up?"

"I've been thinking. About us. Yes, we're having problems, I admit that. And your answer is just to break off and call it a day. My answer is that we sort out the problems ... together."

"There's no point."

"Let me finish. When I left Stuart, you asked me to move in with you. I said no. I was wrong. I see that now. We should be together, to get to know each other properly. Warts and all. Together we can sort everything out. So I agree with you, I should move in with you."

"But I don't want you to move in with me. Not any more." Kevin could see tears forming in her eyes, but he dared not let that weaken his resolve. "It's over, Cath. We're just not right for each other."

"Let's try again, Kev. Once more. Then if it doesn't work out, fine, we'll finish. What do you say?"

"No, Cath. Sorry."

Catherine was sobbing now. "You need time, that's what it is. Time to think things through."

"I have thought ... "

Catherine cut across him. "I'll give you the time, don't worry. As much time as you want. I'll be waiting."

Kevin got up. "I don't believe this. I'm going. So long, Cath." He moved away.

Catherine called after him and when he turned she said, "I'll be waiting."

Kevin left without turning back again. When the door closed behind him, Catherine let the tears flow freely.

* * *

Saturday's game at home to Choreton was to be another with more than its fair share of umpiring problems. The problems started even before the game began. They had only one league umpire for the game, the second umpire having had to cry off that morning owing to illness. So a replacement had to be found.

The obvious one was Doc. He knew the rules inside out and had done a lot of umpiring in his time. But Doc hadn't arrived.

He was usually at the ground some half an hour before a match started in case of any difficulties, but today there was no sign of him.

T.G. phoned Doc's house to find out where he was and Doc's wife told him that her husband had had to take their grandson to the station in Swansea to catch a train after he had been staying the week with them. The boy had originally intended going on the Sunday but there had been a last-minute change of plans. Doc was also going to buy a few things he needed while he was in Swansea, so his wife didn't know what time he'd be back. The only crumb of comfort she could give T.G. was that Doc would be going to the cricket match immediately after getting back.

But that wasn't much comfort. They needed an umpire now.

When T.G. returned from the phone, Clive was talking to Bob. T.G. asked Bob if he would umpire, but Bob gave the same answer he had given Clive earlier. He couldn't as he would be leaving early.

"In that case," T.G. said, "I'll have to do it."

"But you don't umpire, T.G." Clive told him. "You certainly haven't in the time I've been here."

"I used to years ago. It's not something you forget."

Clive paused, trying to think of some alternative. Then he shrugged his shoulders. "We don't have any choice, do we."

What had been worrying Clive was not so much that T.G. hadn't umpired for a long time, but the reason he hadn't umpired for a long time. The captain had a vague recollection of having heard somewhere in the distant past that T.G. should never be allowed to umpire a cricket match, that he had a reputation for being very controversial. It was a reputation that would be enhanced today–and how!

* * *

Clive won the toss and chose to bat. Ian and Pete opened the batting and, although Ian was dismissed early on for only six runs, fears of an immediate collapse were dispelled by a sound second-wicket partnership between Pete and Gary.

It was during this partnership that the problems with the replacement umpire started to become evident. Gary played a ball past the square-leg umpire and as it went towards the boundary, the fielder at mid-wicket set off in pursuit. There should have been three runs in it—and there would have been, except that T.G. signalled one short. According to T.G., Gary's bat hadn't been grounded in the crease at the end of the first run.

"You're joking," Gary told him.

"I do not joke when I'm umpiring," came the emphatic reply.

Gary shook his head in amazement, then dismissed the incident. But he wasn't prepared to be so dismissive when a similar incident occurred four overs later. Again they ran three, again T.G. called one short, again it was Gary who, according to the umpire, was the culprit.

"You do know what you're supposed to be looking for, do you?" Gary asked.

"I know more about cricket than you ever will," T.G. replied.

"In that case, it must be your eyesight that's defective."

"My eyesight is perfect. And I think you'd better watch your tongue, young man."

Gary shook his head, then looking at T.G. asked, "Whose side are you on anyway?" It was a question that would be asked time and again during the course of the match.

Setting aside his dissatisfaction with the umpire, Gary concentrated on his batting again. He and Pete were looking good and the score was moving along nicely.

It was now that the Choreton team began to have cause for dissatisfaction with the umpiring. They changed the bowler at T.G.'s end and in his first over the new bowler was no-balled three times. He accepted the first one quietly, glared at T.G. after the second, and on the third occasion turned to the umpire and asked, "What am I doing wrong, man?"

"Overstepping," T.G. told him and moved forward to indicate where he was going wrong.

The bowler just looked at the Marwen chairman. If looks could kill, T.G. would have been a pool of blood around the stumps.

A Good Catch

The bowler returned to his mark and managed to complete the over without any further no-balls.

But the problem returned in his next over, on the second delivery. The bowler turned on T.G. "Come on, old man, there's got to be something wrong with your eyesight."

T.G. didn't need to reply. Gary, the batsman at the bowler's end, said, "There's nothing wrong with his eyesight, mate. It's your bowling that's faulty. You're overstepping by a mile."

This time it was Gary who was subjected to a glare from the bowler. The latter went back to try again.

"Thank you, Gary," T.G. said quietly. "I'm glad you can see him overstepping too."

"I can't see him overstepping at all, "Gary whispered. "I'm just grateful you're giving us runs as well as taking them off."

The bowler was no-balled again on the last ball of the over. He turned immediately and this time it seemed as if T.G. was in imminent physical danger. But the Choreton captain, fielding at mid-off, went over to tell him to bowl the last ball again and he would then switch him to the other end.

By now the score had moved on to 72. In the next over Pete was caught for 23 and Barry came in. The third wicket pair saw up the 100 and things were looking good for Marwen. Gary had passed his half-century and was hoping for three figures.

The Choreton captain was afraid that these two batsmen would take complete charge, so he brought back one of his opening bowlers at T.G.'s end. The change brought immediate success, thanks to T.G. The third ball of the over pitched in line with the off-stump and cut back, clipping the edge of the bat before hitting Gary on the pad. The bowler, wicket-keeper and a couple of other fielders appealed. T.G. raised his finger.

Gary couldn't believe it. "That hit the bat first," he shouted.

The umpire shook his head.

"You need glasses, T.G."

"No, he doesn't," said a voice coming from behind Gary. It was the bowler who had earlier been no-balled so much and who was now fielding in the slips. Mimicking an Australian accent, he said,

"There's nothing wrong with his eyesight, mate."

Gary could have hit him for that. And he could have hit T.G. He was quite prepared to hit anybody. Very frustrated and very angry, he stormed off, shouting, "No wonder you can't play cricket in this country. If it isn't the weather, it's the bloody umpires."

He didn't bother going to the changing room. When he reached the boundary, he threw his bat to the ground, wrenched off his pads, threw them next to his bat and headed straight for the bar. Right now he needed a lager.

Carl Thomas was the next man in–and the next man out. The first delivery he received struck him high up on the pad. The chances were that the ball would have gone over the stumps. But not in T.G.'s opinion. When the bowler appealed, T.G. gave the batsman out.

After Kevin had come in and taken guard, the slip-fielder who had spoken to Gary told him, "You'd better watch out mate. Your umpire's on a hat-trick. He's going for three l.b.'s in a row. If the ball hits you anywhere below chin level, you've had it."

Kevin concentrated hard and when the bowler sent the ball down it was pitched well up and Kevin got his bat down on it with no trouble. He couldn't help but smile when he heard the slip-fielder say, "He must have given you the benefit of the doubt there."

When the score had moved on to 125, Barry was caught behind for 18 and this time no blame could be attached to T.G. Wickets had now fallen quite quickly since the good second-wicket partnership, too quickly for Clive's liking. He walked to the wicket hoping that he and Kevin could stay together for some time and prevent yet another Marwen collapse. As things turned out, not only did they stay together for some time, but they also put together some fine strokes and pushed the score along at a commendable rate.

This was helped by a change of bowler at T.G.'s end, a youngster coming on to bowl at medium pace. Not that the batsmen were hitting the bowler all over the place. They didn't need to. T.G. kept the score moving by calling "No ball" quite

A Good Catch

regularly—four times in the lad's first over, three in the second. Again the Choreton captain had to change his bowler before too many runs were added to the score—and before T.G. was prematurely added to the local mortality rate.

In the penultimate over Kevin was out, l.b.w., for 31. It was the other umpire who gave this decision, so there was no problem. The score was now 179 for 6.

Steve joined Clive and the pair proceeded to run virtually everything. Although taking risks, neither batsman lost his wicket and Marwen's innings ended with the score at 192 for 6.

* * *

Hardly anyone spoke to T.G. during the tea interval. But that didn't bother him. Umpiring wasn't a popular job and it took a lot of courage to stand up to comments that tended to come from both teams during the course of a game. He had stood up to them during the first innings of today's match and he would continue to do so during the second. Which was just as well, because he continued to give people every reason to make the comments.

The Choreton players were soon to feel aggrieved. Two questionable l.b.w. decisions early in the innings (together with a fine stumping by Arthur) left them on 28 for 3 after nine overs. Inevitably both l.b.w. decisions involved T.G.

At the fall of the third wicket the Choreton captain, Emlyn Harries, came to the wicket. He wasn't at all happy with the situation. He was even less happy ten overs later. Only thirteen runs had been squeezed out of those ten overs with the batsmen almost completely shackled by Marwen's spin attack.

Then Emlyn played forward to a ball from John Price. The ball turned and came off the bat in the direction of forward short leg. It was very close to the ground and Kevin had to dive forward to try to take the catch. The bowler and some of the fielders appealed and T.G. gave the batsman out. Emlyn was certain that the ball had touched the ground first and this was confirmed by Kevin. Even then T.G. was reluctant to reverse his decision, but after Clive had had a word with him he relented.

Two overs later Emlyn was hit on the pad by a ball that had turned so much it must have been missing leg stump. The bowler appealed, the umpire–guess who–raised his finger and Emlyn was out. Before leaving the field, he went to talk to Clive, who was fielding at mid-on. "Listen, Clive, this is becoming a farce. T.G.'s going to win this game for you single-handed. Does he understand the l.b.w. laws?"

"I'll have another word with him," Clive promised and went straight over to the man in question. He took him aside and said, "Cool down on the l.b.'s, T.G. They think you're doing your best to win the game for us. And I must say some of the decisions have been ... well ... close shall we say."

"Are you questioning my ability to make these decisions?"

"I'm just asking for a little discretion, that's all."

"You haven't answered. Are you questioning my ability? Yes or no?"

"Well ... " Clive had to say it. "Yes."

That was it. T.G. took off the white coat and threw it at Clive's feet. He then strode away and headed straight for the bar. He was furious and his fury was increased when he heard the cheers of the Choreton players when they realised what was happening.

Fortunately, by this time Doc had arrived. Clive left the field and went to the Choreton changing room. Emlyn was still in the process of taking off his pads. "Em," Clive said as he entered the room. "T.G.'s decided to give up on the umpiring. But Doc's here now. I take it you've no objection to him taking over.,"

Emlyn spoke quietly. "I'd have no objection to a short-sighted donkey taking over."

"Oh, don't say that, Em" said one of the other Choreton players. "We've already had one short-sighted donkey out there as it is."

Clive made no comment. He went to speak to Doc, who then went out to umpire. There was no further controversy. Doc knew his cricket and was well respected by everyone. If he gave someone out, you could be quite certain he really was out.

Although the change of umpire heartened them, the situation

still looked bleak for Choreton. They were 43 for 4 and in the 21st over. While Clive had been sorting things out, the batsmen had been talking. They decided to try to hit their way out of trouble and wrest the initiative from the bowlers.

Hit out they did and by the end of the 30th over the score was 101 for 4. It even looked possible that Choreton might reach the target of 193 to win.

That likelihood diminished in the next over when John caught and bowled one of the batsmen. The fall of that wicket stemmed the flow of runs, and with Gary taking two wickets in quick succession the score reached only 126 by the 40th over with seven wickets down.

Choreton were now having to hold out for a draw, a task which they duly accomplished with the loss of one further wicket. At the end they were 133 for 8. So, after a very eventful game, the result was a draw. In view of the exceedingly unstable nature of the umpiring, both teams were quite happy with that result.

It was fortunate that both clubs were on such good terms. There would be no complaints, official or otherwise, from Choreton. Had they lost, of course, the situation would probably have been different. But they hadn't, so they were prepared to let the matter go. The relationship between the two clubs would remain as amicable as ever.

* * *

Within the Marwen club, however, amicability was far from complete. T.G. was sitting in the far corner of the clubhouse, not wanting anything to do with anybody–other than the person who was serving him all the double whiskies he was drinking.

Jessica had tried to talk to him. "Don't take it to heart, Dad," she told him. "Clive didn't mean it."

With the whisky beginning to affect his speech, her father replied, "Yes he did. He doesn't think I can ummmmm . . . pire. None of them do. Well if that's what they thhhhhh . . . ink, I'll give up ummmmmm . . . piring. And what's more I'll give up being ch . . . ch . . . chairman of the club. I'm reeeeee . . . signing."

"Don't be silly, Dad. You can't resign. They'd have to close the place if you packed in."

T.G. shook his head. "Nobody's irrep...irrep...They'll get by."

"Impossible!"

"Thank you for your loyalty, my dear. But if you don't mind, I'd like to be left alone to get commm...pletely puddled and fffff...orget everything and every...body."

Jessica could see there was no point trying to reason with her father now, so she left him to get on with drowning his sorrows.

* * *

When Clive came into the clubhouse after changing, Jessica told him about her conversation with her father. He immediately went over to T.G. "And what do you think you're doing over here on your own?" he asked.

"Getting drrrrrr...unk," came the reply. "At least you can't quuuuuu...estion my ability to do that."

"Come on, T.G.," said Clive as he sat down. "I didn't mean anything personal out there. It was just...Well...We've all got our limitations and we should accept them. There are some things you can do well, some things I can do well. We should stick to those."

"And what thhhhhhh...ings can I do well?"

"Keep this club ticking over for one thing. So let's have no talk of resigning. Right?"

"I...have...reeeee...signed."

"Not until you put it in writing. And you couldn't even write your name in this state.,"

"Give me aaaa...a pen."

"No. You can do that on Monday if you'll still want to resign then."

"I wwwwww...ill.

"Now let me show you something I can do well. Firstly, I can get a double whisky for the chairman. And after that I can get another one if he wants. Does that impress you?"

A Good Catch

"Undoubt . . . Undoubt . . . Yes."

"Only one thing though. I'll be putting the glasses on the table over there with the lads. If you want those drinks you'll have to sit over there with us."

T.G. looked at Clive. Well, actually he was looking at two Clives. This wasn't an indication that he was getting more drunk. It was, in fact, an indication that he was getting more sober because at the start of the conversation he could see three Clives.

The chairman allowed one of the Clives—he couldn't tell which—to lead him over to the main group and put him in a chair there. After two more doubles T.G. noticed that there were three Clives again. After another double he didn't notice anything.

It took one Clive and one Kevin to take T.G. out to Jessica's car. The two players went in the car as well and later helped Jessica get her father to bed.

T.G. didn't wake up until eleven o' clock the following morning and when he did wake up he wasn't feeling particularly well. Later in the day he and Jessica had a long talk about the events of the previous day. He informed her of two important decisions he had made. Firstly, he was not going to give up the chairmanship; secondly, he was going to give up drinking whisky. The first decision was confirmed at Monday evening's committee meeting; the second was rescinded at the same meeting.

Chapter 10

A BAD DAY'S NIGHT

Although the match against Choreton had been drawn, Marwen had been in the ascendancy and this, allied to their two victories in the previous matches, had left the players in a celebratory mood. The avoidance of relegation was now much more than a distant possibility.

While T.G. had been sitting in his drunken stupor on Saturday evening, he missed all the plans that were being made for a 'stayer' the following week. The team would be playing at Brynteg and only a few weeks previously a new night club had opened in Brynteg. The club was quite near the cricket ground, so this would be an ideal opportunity for a good night out. Everyone was in favour and it was decided to hire a minibus to take them to and from Brynteg so that there would be no drink-driving problems.

"What about the women?" John asked.

"There'll be plenty of those there," Ian replied.

"I mean our women. Are we taking them?"

"I thought we were supposed to be planning a good night out. Why spoil it?"

"They'll probably want to come."

"Tough."

It was decided that they would all put their foot down on this and make it a men-only event. But they would have to tell their wives and girlfriends first, so they wouldn't finalise arrangements until that particular hurdle had been overcome. They would all meet again at the club on Tuesday evening.

When Clive told Pat about the planned night out, she thought it was an excellent idea. When he told her it was to be men only, she informed him of one man who would not be going.

Similar conversations took place in other houses in the Marwen area over the weekend and the result of the men's decision to put their foot down regarding this matter was that the women would be going with them on the trip. Everyone would go to Brynteg in time for the match and while the men would be playing, the women would either watch or go for a walk. They would probably opt for the latter and have a picnic somewhere.

* * *

On Saturday morning Gary informed Clive that he wouldn't be going in the minibus with the others. He'd find his own way to the Brynteg ground.

"But you haven't got a car," Clive said. "And you don't know where the ground is. You don't even know where Brynteg is. You've never been there."

"No problem," said Gary. "A friend of mine'll drive me there and she knows the way."

"She? Who's this then?"

Gary picked up his kit-bag and went to the door. "I'll introduce you tonight," he said and left.

Clive wondered who the poor girl was. Gary hadn't got in until the early hours of the morning and here he was, going out to see her again. This wasn't in line with his usual one-night stand approach. And she must have been really drunk to have agreed to go out with him again. Clive smiled. But she'll have sobered up by now, so she'll probably just stand him up. That'll pull him down a peg or two, especially as he's said beforehand that he's taking her. The smile turned to a frown. If she does stand him up, how's he going to get there?

* * *

Clive needn't have worried. By the time the minibus arrived at Brynteg's ground at five past one, Gary had already arrived. So she hadn't stood him up. Poor girl, thought Clive again.

The reason for the earlier arrival at the ground was that, with the evenings drawing in, matches in the latter part of the season started at one thirty instead of two o' clock.

The men went to change, the women picked up their picnic bags to take with them on their walk. Shortly before the men took to the field ready to play, the women were making their way out of the ground. As things turned out that day, it would probably have been better had the women taken to the field and the men had gone for a walk.

They knew from the outset that this would be a difficult game. Brynteg were top of the table and looking set for promotion. But Marwen themselves were playing much better now, so they hoped they would give the top team a good run for its money. Little did they know. Brynteg won the toss and batted first. Knowing that Marwen used two spin bowlers from the outset, the Brynteg captain changed his batting order. The two usual openers were much less comfortable facing spin than they were facing fast bowlers, so they were moved down the order. Opening the batting today would be the captain himself, Pete Stringer, and the wicket-keeper, Jim Hobson. Both were very experienced players and it was felt that they would be able to cope better than most with Marwen's spin attack.

Cope they did and the 50 came up without loss in the fifteenth over. This was due to a dogged determination on the part of the batsmen to assert themselves over the Marwen spinners. But it was also due in no small part to a re-appearance of the disease that had plagued Marwen for so long this season. Yes, they were dropping catches again.

Jim Hobson was the main beneficiary, being dropped three times in those first fifteen overs, once by Steve in the slips, once by Andy at mid-off and once by Ian at long-on. The third chance was the easiest. Jim hit the ball straight and high. Very high. Ian came running in to take the catch, but he completely miscued the trajectory and ran in too far. By the time he realised where the ball was going, it was too late. He ran back to try to retrieve the situation, but the chance was gone. He got only his finger-tips to the ball.

Had this been a Test match, Ian could have claimed that he lost the ball in the crowd. Had there been some trees around the ground, he could have claimed that he lost the ball in the trees. Had he not been daydreaming when the ball had been hit, he wouldn't have needed to look for any excuses.

Pete Stringer had given a sharp caught-and-bowled chance to Gary, but that too had gone down. Kevin couldn't resist the opportunity to make a comment. "I'm glad it wasn't anybody else who dropped that."

"Listen, mate," the Australian replied. "I made that into a chance. None of you lot would have got your hands to it."

"Yes, but don't forget, we're only Poms. We're expected to do that. But you ... you're an Aussie."

Before Gary could reply, Clive shouted, "OK, you two. That's enough. Get on with the game." Clive would be glad when this particular season was over. Keeping the peace between Gary and his team-mates was proving to be increasingly difficult.

Another difficult task was trying to contain the Brynteg batsmen, who were looking very comfortable indeed. The 100 came up in the 27th over and after thirty overs the score was 114 for no wicket.

Clive had given the spinners long enough to break through—perhaps too long—but it was evidently not to be their day, so he made a double bowling change, bringing on Andy in place of Gary and Steve instead of John. The captain hoped that the bowlers who had opened the attack earlier in the season would have more success than the current opening bowlers. But it wasn't to be their day either. Steve, in particular, was given a very hard time, his five overs costing 36 runs, so he was replaced by Carl.

Andy fared a little better—but only a little—his first five overs costing 25 runs. But he did manage to claim a wicket in his fifth over. Jim Hobson was bowled by a yorker, having scored 89.

After forty overs Brynteg were 177 for 1 with Pete Stringer still there on 80. For that fact he could thank the fielders who had dropped him twice more after the difficult chance given to Gary.

So the dropped catches disease was back with a vengeance—and if they thought it had been bad thus far, there was much worse to come. With plenty of wickets in hand, Brynteg set about the bowling with even greater ferocity over the last ten overs. They hit out at almost everything, hitting the ball hard and high and hoping Marwen would put down any possible chances.

Marwen duly obliged, the situation almost degenerating into farce. It got to the point where a player would go for a catch with no-one expecting him to take it. Ten chances went down in the last ten overs, half of them being put down by Ian, who also managed to mis-field seven times in that period. It was as if the ball was following him. Clive would move him out of harm's way—or so he thought—but almost immediately the ball would go where he had moved him.

The others (apart from Gary) felt really sorry for Ian, but were really glad that it was he, not they, who was being subjected to this. Had they played with a live grenade, they couldn't have dreaded its appearance in their vicinity much more than they did today's match ball.

When the innings ended after fifty overs, Brynteg had amassed 243 for 1, with Pete Stringer 121 not out. They had gained an amazing six batting points while Marwen had failed to pick up even one bowling point.

The fielders were glad to come off. They consoled themselves with the fact that Brynteg were top of the table and on their way to the First Division. But that didn't excuse them for all those dropped catches. Oh, those dropped catches!

* * *

That Brynteg were almost certainly going to gain promotion was due mainly to two factors. The first was the solidity of their batting. Not once had the batting crumbled this season. It could virtually be guaranteed that one batsman or another would succeed each week—and usually it was two or three who succeeded. They had secured more batting points thus far this season than any team in any of the four divisions of the league.

The other major factor in their success was Lester Woodford, their opening bowler. His parents hailed from Barbados, but Lester had been born in London and had lived in Britain all of his twenty-one years. The last two of those had been spent in Brynteg, where he, his wife and their baby son had settled.

It was Brynteg Cricket Club's good fortune that he had moved there. He had joined the club towards the end of last season and had been with them from the outset this year. And what an impact he was making! He was easily the fastest bowler in the Second Division and had twice taken seven wickets in an innings this season.

He had missed the previous game against Marwen owing to illness, a stomach complaint that had kept him out of cricket for three weeks, but since his return he had shown himself to be as effective as ever.

None of the Marwen bowlers had seen him bowl before. They didn't see much of him today either. The wickets fell steadily and the innings was all over in about eighty minutes. At one point Marwen were 10 for 5 (and two of those were byes). The scorebook made depressing reading as far as Marwen were concerned:

I. Cowling b. Woodford 0

P. Richards l.b.w. b. Woodford 1

G. Hudson b. Woodford 2

B. Roberts b. Woodford 5

C. Thomas l.b.w. b. Woodford 0

They simply had no answer to this exceptional bowler. Each batsman in turn had gone to the wicket determined to play himself in, take no chances and be especially careful as far as Woodford was concerned. That was the plan. Then each batsman in turn, on his way back to the pavilion, had had to reflect on how the plan had gone wrong.

Kevin and Clive were now together at the wicket and although neither was very comfortable out there, at least they had both stayed out there.

With the five wickets that had fallen so far, only one player had been involved. Woodford had either bowled the batsman or trapped him l.b.w.. None of the fielders had been involved. Not one batsman had been out caught. Could it be perhaps that Brynteg's catching wasn't up to much? Or was it just a coincidence that none of the wickets so far had been a catch?

It was just a coincidence—as Kevin found out when he was caught behind off Woodford for 13. As if to hammer the point home, Steve was also caught behind off the same bowler two deliveries later. Marwen were 34 for 7.

John came in, glad that it was the end of the over and that he didn't have to face Woodford yet. With luck, Clive would get to the 'danger area' before the start of Woodford's next over.

Clive scored two runs off the first ball of the next over but, try as he might, he was unable to get any runs off the other five balls. Of course, for their part, Brynteg were determined to keep Clive where he was so that Woodford would have the opportunity to bowl at John. They succeeded and so John would now be in the thick of the action.

A draught near his nose told him that the first ball had gone by. A similar draught a minute or so later indicated that the second ball had gone by as well. John concentrated hard. He might have to play the next ball.

The third ball came and John played forward to it. Again it went past him. He also played forward to the next ball, which caught the edge of the bat and flew between first and second slips. Four runs. John played forward to the fifth ball as well. Again it caught the edge of the bat, but this time went between second and third slips. Four more runs.

This is ridiculous, John thought to himself. What am I? A man or a mouse? He determined to move on to the attack. He launched himself into the next stroke, intending to drive the ball

A Good Catch

through the covers. Second slip launched himself to his right to catch the ball, which had again come off the edge of John's bat. This time the catch was taken and John was on his way back to the pavilion. 44 for 8.

Lester Woodford had taken all eight wickets to fall. Could he manage to take all ten?

Arthur was the next batsman in and he and Clive added twelve runs very, very carefully. When he had been facing Woodford, Arthur had concentrated hard, determined to halt the bowler's run of success. It was a pity he didn't concentrate equally hard when he was at the other end. The other bowler trapped him l.b.w. for 5.

Andy was the last man in and he was glad he was away from the danger end. He didn't want to face Woodford. He didn't have to. He was bowled first ball.

Marwen were all out for 56, with Clive not out 17. In a match in which Brynteg had secured 23 points, Marwen had picked up only one. The performance was nothing short of pathetic and, with only two matches to go before the end of the season, relegation had again become a distinct possibility.

* * *

The Marwen players were deflated. They were in no mood to go to a night club tonight. They couldn't have chosen a worse day to go there.

Of course, another way of looking at it was that this was the best day to go. They could forget all about today's game, forget about the miserable season, forget about cricket full stop. They could simply concentrate on having a good time. Drink, drink and more drink, without a cricket ball in sight. Yes, perhaps this was the ideal time to have such a night.

Such thinking lifted the mood in the changing room and by the time they joined the women in the clubhouse the players were in better spirits. They would have a few drinks here before moving on.

Gary wasn't with them. He had changed quickly and left,

stating he would join them in the night club later on. The chance of having some time away from the Australian was most welcome. One of the players even suggested they should now change their plans and go to a different night club.

After staying in the Brynteg clubhouse for almost three hours—as the drinks were cheaper there—the Marwen party moved on to the night club, which was called "Sparklers".

Gary hadn't arrived yet. For which they were all grateful. They moved some tables closer together so that the whole group could be together. They split themselves into rounds and Clive was the first to get the drinks in his particular round. When he came back, he warned the others, "If you've forgotten your credit cards, you'd better leave now. The water here is more expensive than the beer back home."

* * *

Although they didn't particularly want the Australian's company, the group from Marwen did find themselves looking forward to Gary's arrival to some extent in order to meet his companion. What would she be like? Would they know her?

They knew her alright. When Gary came in, he was closely followed by Catherine Wilkins. The others looked at her in stunned silence, then looked straight towards the bar where Kevin was standing, buying drinks. This might not, after all, be a particularly good night.

Gary took Catherine over to the group and having found her a chair went to the bar. Kevin was paying for his drinks and hadn't seen Gary coming.

"Good day! Good day! Good day!" the Australian said.

Kevin turned, knowing already who had spoken. In a far from welcoming tone he said, "Oh, you've arrived."

"Yep. Well spotted, Kev." He put his arm on Kevin's shoulder. "And I've brought a friend." He turned Kevin round and pointed him towards where Catherine was sitting.

"You bastard!" Kevin said. "What did you bring her for?"

"We've become good friends, Cath and me. You don't mind,

do you?"

"You've got to stir up trouble, haven't you?"

"Nothing of the sort, my friend. She's a free agent now." Gary smiled. "Don't tell me you're still interested."

Kevin glared at his antagonist, then picked up the drinks and left him. Had he stayed, he couldn't have kept his hands off the grinning Aussie. He went to his table, nodding to Catherine as he went past her. He was glad he was sitting far enough away from her. He'd be even more glad when this evening was over. He was beginning to wish he hadn't come.

After a while various members of the group took to the dance floor. Others preferred to concentrate on the drinking. Kevin wished Jessica was here now so that he could stay with her the whole evening. She had been playing for the Seconds today, having decided to have another go at playing cricket, and she didn't feel like driving over to Brynteg afterwards. Kevin thought it strange that he was thinking about Jessica. He never used to.

His thoughts were interrupted by Catherine. "Would you mind dancing with me, Kevin? Gary's a little tied up with his drinking at the moment."

Not wanting to create a scene, Kevin got up and accompanied Catherine to the dance floor. As they danced she said, "You don't look pleased to see me, Kev."

"Why should I be?"

"That's not a nice thing to say. Especially as I came here just to see you."

"You came here with the kangaroo."

"Oh, he was just my invite card. I'd heard you were all coming to this place, so I needed some way of getting here myself. There's no need for you to worry, Kev. I've got no interest in him at all. Credit me with some sense, please."

When the music ended, Kevin made to leave the dance floor, but Catherine asked him for one more dance. This time the music was much slower and they danced close together. Kevin could smell that perfume she had worn on their first nights out together. Those first wonderful nights. They danced quietly for a while, both lost in their own thoughts. Then Kevin whispered in her ear, "It's not going to work, Cath."

"What are you talking about?" she asked.

"You're trying to get me back. I've told you, it's all over between us."

"You can't blame me for trying."

"I wish you wouldn't."

"Sorry, Kev. You know how stubborn I can be."

After the dance they went back to their respective seats. They didn't dance together again that night. Kevin made sure of that by dancing with every other woman in their group and a few others besides. Catherine was amused at this. It didn't bother her at all, she had done what she wanted. She had let him know that she wouldn't give up. OK, so he didn't want her tonight. But there'd be other nights. As she had told him, she could be very stubborn.

In the meantime, after imbibing a substantial quantity of lager, Gary took to the dance floor—with Pat. As he held her close to him, he whispered to her, "Have I ever told you how attractive you are?"

"Don't start that again," she told him.

He had tried to start conversations like this before, but she had put him firmly in his place every time. This time, however, he'd had a lot more to drink and was determined to have his say. "Clive doesn't appreciate you as he should. I bet he doesn't tell you how attractive you are. Well, I'm telling you. And I'll tell you again, some day when he's at work I'll . . ."

Pat pushed him away and went straight back to Clive. Gary went to the Gents. It wasn't long before Clive followed him there.

"Hi there, skip," Gary said. "Enjoying yourself?"

Clive said nothing until he had pinned Gary up against the wall. "I'm not usually a violent man," he said. "I don't believe that violence solves anything. But with you I might make an exception."

Gary went to say something, but Clive, his face very close to that of the Australian, told him, "Don't say a word. Just listen. I've had enough of you and your stunts. More than enough. You fancy yourself with the women. OK, that's your concern. But when you try it on with my wife, it's my concern.

"That may be the way of life in Australia. But you're living in Marwen now and we tend to be a bit more civilised here. Seems you're having difficulty adjusting to that. Tough." He tightened his grip. "Cos adjust you've got to. It's been hell having you staying with us, but I've put up with it for the sake of the club. But you talk to Pat like that again and that's it, you're out, you find somewhere else to stay. And take it from me, you'd be damned lucky to find anybody who'd take you."

Clive let him go, then turned and walked out.

The whole scenario was watched by a well-built man washing his hands. When Gary saw him looking, he shrugged his shoulders and laughed. The man came up to him and said, "If that had been me, I'd have put you through that wall." Then he left.

A few minutes later, Gary emerged from the toilets and saw a redhead sitting alone at a nearby table. Had he used a modicum of sense, he would have realised that she had probably come with someone and that that someone was buying drinks or some such thing. Gary, however, wasn't particularly well-endowed with sense, so he went over to the girl and said, "You don't know me, but I think you should."

Before she could answer, her companion returned with the drinks he had been fetching and put them on the table. It was the man Gary had seen in the Gents. "Do you know this berk?" he asked the girl.

"No," she replied, "but he thinks I should."

With that, the man turned Gary round and hit him hard in the stomach. This really winded the Australian. Before Gary had a chance to realise what was happening, the man delivered a right hook of which any boxer would have been proud and the recipient of said right hook was on the floor, blood pouring from his mouth.

Before the man could get hold of Gary again, he was held back by two men from the next table. Ian and Carl came over to lift Gary up and take him to their table. The man shouted at

Gary, "And you'd better keep your distance or next time I'll finish the job."

"I don't think he likes me," Gary said as the others put him to sit down.

Clive came over and told Catherine, "I think it would be best if you took him out now. Before anything really serious happens."

Catherine got up. "You must be joking. I'm not putting up with him any more. You can keep him. He's all yours." She walked out without saying another word.

They had put Gary to sit in the middle of the group. This prevented him from going round the club and causing trouble. But it didn't prevent him from talking incessantly and getting on everybody's nerves. It wasn't long before they decided that the best thing to do was leave. It was a little after midnight. They had intended staying later but, in view of the circumstances, they changed their minds.

As the others headed for the door, Kevin went to the bar and bought a double whisky. He took the drink to the man who had decked Gary. "Here you are, mate. And thanks a lot." He said no more, but just walked away to catch up with the others.

The man looked after him in amazement. He couldn't understand it. That was the fourth member of that group who had bought him a drink tonight.

* * *

Having already spoilt what should have been a good night, Gary now proceeded to spoil the journey home as well. Ten minutes into the journey, he wanted the bus to stop so that he could relieve himself. Clive told him they weren't going to stop. Gary appealed to the others for support but they all ignored him. He then got down on his knees in front of Clive and begged him to stop the bus. When that failed, he got up and announced, "If you don't stop this bus right now, I'll do it here in front of everybody."

"Don't be so stupid," Clive told him. "We've only got about six miles to go."

"I don't care," Gary said and started to unzip his trousers.

A Good Catch

"OK, OK," Clive said and asked the driver to stop the bus.

The bus pulled over to the side of the road and Gary got off. Steve now got up and said he might as well take advantage of the opportunity rather than wait, but Clive told him to sit down. Then the captain closed the door and told the driver to drive on. The bus moved off, leaving Gary to walk back after watering the hedge.

Chapter 11

THE LONG ARM OF THE LAW

It was a bad weekend all round for Kevin. The 'big night' at Brynteg had turned sour. Then on the Sunday he was stopped by the police and breathalysed.

He had gone out for a drink with Bob and, rather than go down to the cricket club as they usually did, they had gone in Kevin's car to a pub about six miles away, not far from the spot where Gary had been left the previous night.

Kevin had just wanted to go out for a quiet drink and talk to Bob about the problems he was having with Catherine. They had talked and Bob had told him to carry on as he had been doing so far, not giving Catherine any hope regarding getting back together and waiting for her to face facts and give in.

Then the conversation moved on to the situation between Bob and Carol, how Carol kept dropping hints about an engagement and how Bob had so far kept ignoring those hints.

"I suppose we'll get engaged eventually," Bob said, then paused before adding, "and we might even get engaged to each other."

The two men laughed, then Kevin warned. "You'd better not leave it too late or else our Australian friend will move in on Carol. She must be the only female in the village he hasn't tried it on with."

Bob laughed again. "Can you picture what would happen if he did try anything?"

Kevin also laughed at the prospect. "There wouldn't be much left of him. I suppose he must have more sense than I've given him credit for."

And so the evening went on, with the two of them discussing various matters, usually in a light-hearted manner. It was just the sort of evening Kevin needed. The talking and laughing took so much of their attention that they hardly did any drinking. Two pints each were all they had.

This turned out to be most fortunate for Kevin because on their way back to Marwen they were stopped by a police car. The rear off-side brake light on Kevin's car wasn't working and while the policeman was talking to Kevin about this he could smell alcohol on his breath. Kevin assured him that he had had only two pints, but the policeman insisted on breathalysing him.

Kevin hoped that all he had drunk the previous night had got out of his system. He blew into the breathalyser and handed it back nervously to the constable. The test was negative.

"You do understand, sir," said the constable. "We can't be too careful. And there was the smell of alcohol on your breath."

"No, I do not understand, officer," said Kevin. "You've caused me a great deal of concern."

"There's no need to feel concern if you're in the clear, sir."

"I told you I'd only had two pints."

"Everybody says that."

"So you don't believe anybody, is that it?"

"If everybody could be believed, there wouldn't be a need for so many policemen."

"Don't you trust anybody?"

"Only honest people, sir."

"Don't I look honest?"

"I'd rather not answer that, sir."

"I object to that."

Bob intervened before Kevin talked himself into trouble. "Come off it, Kev. Even your mother wouldn't say you had an honest face. If I didn't know you so well, I wouldn't trust you myself."

Kevin looked at Bob, then laughed.

"You can go now, sir," the policeman told him. "But get that light seen to quickly."

The policeman walked back towards the patrol car. Kevin, relieved at the result of the test, told Bob, "Come on. I need a drink after that." The policeman heard this and turned, so Kevin added. "After parking the car, of course," then waved to the constable.

Kevin drove back to Marwen at a steady 30 miles per hour. After parking the car outside his house, he and Bob went straight down to the cricket club. This time the drinking was given greater priority. If he'd been breathalysed now, Kevin wouldn't have stood a chance.

* * *

Later on in the week Kevin again found himself in confrontation with the police. On Monday evening Clive phoned him to ask if he could play in a hastily arranged friendly match on Wednesday evening starting at six o' clock. The match had been arranged in order to give the Marwen team some extra practice before their two remaining League fixtures. The opponents? Llanelli Police.

The team for the Ramley match on Saturday wouldn't be announced until after Wednesday's game. Clive told Kevin that while his place was quite secure, some players would be playing for their places on Wednesday.

"Is it only coppers from Llanelli who'll be playing?" Kevin asked.

Clive told him he thought they were going to get some players from surrounding areas but mainly it would be Llanelli policemen.

"I hope the sod who breathalysed me is playing," Kevin said. "I can get my own back then."

"I don't know exactly which sods are playing, Kev. All I know is that there'll be eleven of them and the game's on Wednesday."

"I'll be there."

* * *

A Good Catch

In fact, ten of last Saturday's team were there. Only Andy Jones couldn't make it. He was away on a course for the week, though he would be back in time for Saturday's match.

The only change from the team that played Brynteg was Jessica in place of Andy. It was hoped she might regain some of her confidence playing with the others again. Kevin laughed when T.G. told him this. "Playing with the rest of us is one sure way of not regaining her confidence," he said.

It was also hoped that in a match which was not a League fixture the whole team might relax and get their act together. They could play now knowing there were no points at stake. With that pressure off, the performance would surely be better. As if!!!

* * *

Gary was looking forward to the game. He had got to know some of the policemen in Llanelli quite well by now, having already spent two nights in the cells there and receiving countless warnings from various officers who had encountered him on their beats.

The policemen themselves couldn't stand him. He was trouble wherever he went and his condescending attitude towards the police in general didn't endear him to them at all. As far as they were concerned, if ever there was a case for deportation, this was it.

The policemen in their cricket team were looking forward to this hastily arranged game as it would give them a chance to sort out the Australian on the field. The batsmen were looking forward to hitting the Aussie's bowling all over the place, while the bowlers were just looking forward to bowling at him. Not to him, but at him.

* * *

The police team played only a few matches each year. Four of the players played cricket each week in one league or another, but the others just enjoyed playing these friendlies, mainly because of the good nights that tended to follow.

On arriving at Marwen's ground the first person they saw, inevitably, was Gary. He was walking up the drive as the three cars turned into the drive. Bill Sefton, the driver of the first car, was tempted to drive straight at him, but decided against it as it might damage the car.

"Hi there, boys," Gary shouted as the policemen got out of the cars. "I see you've come to pick up some tips on how to play cricket."

Bill wondered whether it might have been worth damaging the car after all.

Gary joined them. "Now it's my turn to show you some hospitality. And I'm only too glad to do it after all your kindnesses to me in the past. And in the future too, no doubt."

Bill told him. "Shut up, Hudson and show us where we change."

"Certainly, Bill, my boy, certainly," said Gary. He led them to their changing room and talked all the way there. They were glad to slam the door shut, leaving their 'friend' outside, still talking. All the players pleaded with Colin Wilson, their captain, for a chance to bowl at the Australian, even ones who didn't usually bowl. "Just one over. That's all I'll need."

* * *

Wilson won the toss and decided to bat first. Opening the batting were Bill Sefton and Mike Bembridge, the latter being the one who had stopped Kevin on Sunday. As the batsmen walked out, Kevin noticed his favourite policeman and went towards him. "Victimised any good drivers lately?" he asked.

Mike was quick with his reply. "I never stop good drivers, only bad ones."

Mike then went to the bowler's end, where he immediately recognised the umpire as the passenger in Kevin's car on Sunday. Bob had told Carol that he was going down to watch the game for a short while, but when he arrived at the ground Clive begged him to umpire with Doc. He pointed out that the only alternative, apart from the players themselves doing it, was T.G. Bob agreed to help, though he knew someone who wouldn't be particularly pleased about that. Still, she'd understand after he explained to her ... Well, perhaps she would.

* * *

Clive decided to change his opening attack for this game in order to try out another possibility. Instead of starting with two spinners, he would use spin at one end and medium pace at the other. Gary would bowl the first over, with Steve bowling at the other end.

Bill Sefton had taken guard and was looking at the field placings when Gary shouted, "Hey, Bill, I'll bowl underarm if you like. To give you a chance of hitting the ball."

"You bowl any way you like," the batsman replied. "Hitting the ball won't be a problem."

At last the game started. Bill played forward to the first three deliveries and each time the ball hit the middle of the bat. The fourth ball was a bad one, a long-hop, and Bill gave it the treatment it deserved, sending it to the mid-wicket boundary. He took a single off the last ball of the over, so that he was down at the bowler's end when Bob signalled the end of the over. "I thought you could bowl," Bill told Gary.

Gary wasn't amused. "Haven't warmed up yet, mate. You wait."

Steve's bad run continued in this game. His first over cost eight runs, his second ten. Gary's second over cost six runs, but there was also a missed chance. Mike Bembridge hit the ball in the direction of mid-on. Barry, fielding a little deep, ran for it. Gary also ran for it. Clive could see what was coming, so too could everyone else other than Barry and Gary. Neither of the two called, so they ended up running into each other and the ball ended up on the ground.

"Couldn't you see me going for it?" yelled Gary.

"That was my catch, you pillock," Barry yelled back

Clive came towards them from mid-off. "It's no use shouting now. You should have been using your voices earlier. Call for the damn thing if you're going for it. Don't just run in like dummies."

Barry and Gary glared at each other, then Clive shouted at

them to get on with the game.

Steve conceded another eight runs in his third over, so Clive had to take him off and bring John on in his place.

The batsmen were well on top and at the halfway stage of the twenty-over innings the Police were 58 for no wicket. Gary was coming in for some punishment now, so Clive decided to give him a rest and bring Pete on instead. Normally in a twenty-over game there would in any case have been a limit to the number of overs each bowler could bowl, but both sides had agreed to do without such a restriction in this game.

After twelve overs the score was 65 for no wicket and there was no sign of a breakthrough. It was in the thirteenth over that John, having seen that they couldn't bowl the batsmen out, decided to talk the batsmen out. The second ball of the over was of good length, yet Mike Bembridge drove it through the covers for four runs. "What on earth do you think you're doing?" John asked him. With the batsman looking at him bemused, John went on, "I don't mind you hitting the bad balls for four, but you leave the good ones alone. Treat them with the respect they deserve." With that John winked at Arthur, but the batsman didn't notice it.

Bembridge was amazed at the bowler's conceit. He knew that Gary was arrogant, but here was another one. He'd teach him a lesson now. He knew what he was going to do with the big head's next ball.

John and Arthur had a good idea of what the batsman intended to do. But they also knew what John intended to do. The batsman didn't, so he was out next ball. As John came up to bowl, Bembridge prepared to go down the wicket and hit him out of the ground. John saw him moving and bowled the ball faster down the leg side, where Arthur was waiting for it. The batsman was well out of his crease when Arthur whipped off the bails. (Such a ball down the leg side could have been called a wide in a limited-over game, but such technicalities were not observed in this 'friendly'.)

The scorebook read that "M. Bembridge st. A. Howells b. J. Price 29." It should have read: "M. Bembridge conned J. Price 29."

Colin Wilson, the captain, was the new batsman. He played

A Good Catch

cricket for Staylings, a team in the Third Division of the League, the division in which Marwen could well be playing next year.

John called Barry in from long-on. "There's no need to stay out there, Barry. He won't try and hit it that far."

The comment was noted by the batsman—as it was meant to be. Wilson played defensive shots to the first two deliveries he received. Then he thought he'd go for a big one before the fielders were pushed back again. But John had previously told Barry to drop back a few paces after each ball, so when Wilson went for the big drive off the fifth ball of the over Barry was well positioned to take the catch.

Seeing the possibility of a collapse, Bill Sefton went on the offensive in the next over and hit Pete for three fours and a two. In contrast, John's next over was a maiden. So after fifteen overs the score was 83 for 2.

Clive now brought Gary back, believing that the batsmen might now be beginning to worry about the spin bowling. They were indeed more wary now and with this psychological advantage, Gary and John picked up more wickets, and by the end of the allotted twenty overs the Police had scored 98 for 7. Most of the runs in the last eight overs were scored by Bill Sefton, who finished on 57 not out.

Bill was warmly applauded as he left the field. Even Gary praised him. "Good on yer, mate. A bit lucky, but good nonetheless."

The luck to which he was referring concerned three dropped catches in the last couple of overs. Ian dropped two and Carl the other.

Only one other catch was taken after Barry's. That was when Jessica ran in from mid-on to take a diving catch off Gary's bowling. Gary was impressed and put his arm around her as he congratulated her.

Jessica thought to herself, "Either he's unwell or he's after my body."

Kevin thought to himself, He must be unwell and he's after her body."

* * *

Marwen's innings started the usual way. Ian was out for a duck and Pete for 2. Not for the first time this season, it was up to Gary and Barry to halt the slide. They got down to the task well and put on 39 runs for the third wicket. It would have been more had Gary not gone out to an excellent catch by Bill Sefton.

Trevor Denton was bowling. He had already taken the two wickets to fall and had provided problems for the present batsmen early on in their partnership. But they had weathered the storm and were coping well. Colin Wilson told Trevor to have one more over, then he would take him off.

It was in that over that the catch occurred. The ball pitched in line with leg stump and Gary clipped it backward of square. Bill, fielding at square-leg, dived full length to his right to pull off a truly remarkable catch. Gary had been sure it would be two runs at least, yet he was now out. Had Bill's reach been slightly shorter, he wouldn't have got his hand to the ball. Gary told him as he walked past, "Now I know what they mean by the long arm of the law."

In the next over Barry was out l.b.w. for 17 and Marwen's batting folded again. Carl was out for a duck, Clive for 1 and Steve for 1. Trevor Denton, who had been kept on following Gary's dismissal, took two of those wickets.

With Marwen on 48 for 7 in the middle of the fifteenth over, Jessica came to the wicket to join Kevin. She played out the over without any problems, then went down the wicket to talk to Kevin.

He told her that they would now have to push the score along. They had nothing to lose. They couldn't do worse than the others. But all they could manage in the next over was a single off every ball. The Police team were quite content for them to have this as six runs an over wouldn't take Marwen to their target.

Jessica and Kevin held another conference at the end of the over. "Let's put some pressure on the fielders" was Jessica's suggestion. They returned to their positions and now the fun started.

With four overs to go, 45 runs were still needed for victory.

A Good Catch

They needed boundaries, but try as they did, they managed only one in those four overs—a glorious off-drive by Jessica.

Boundaries there may not have been, but excitement there was and that in abundance. What went on in those four overs had to be seen to be believed. They were running two runs where really there was only one. Whether the ball hit bat or pad, they ran. Wherever the ball went, they ran. With the wicket-keeper standing back, even if the ball went through to him, they ran.

And they got away with it. In trying to hurry, fielders either fumbled the ball or, if they did manage to pick it up, threw it wildly and nowhere near the stumps.

But it looked all over in the penultimate over. Again they tried running two where there was only one run. Jessica was hurrying back to the wicket-keeper's end and the wicket-keeper was waiting for the throw from the fielder who had the ball in his hand. The throw came in and Jessica was still only halfway down the wicket. She knew it was all over but kept running anyway.

It was a good job she did. The wicket-keeper was so relieved that this partnership was at last to be broken that he lost his concentration for one split second and in that split second he dropped the ball. Jessica was back in the crease before he recovered it—and she heard every word he said, including some words that were completely new to her.

In spite of this gallant effort by Kevin (21 not out) and Jessica (18 not out), Marwen failed to reach their target. After their twenty overs they were 90 for 7. They had lost again and this time to a team that wasn't even in the League.

* * *

A defeat like this was the last thing they wanted now. The game had been arranged to try and help them prepare for the final push to avoid relegation. Yet far from helping them, the game seemed to have set them back. A number of batsmen had failed completely and the dropped catches were as prevalent as ever.

One good thing in all this was Jessica's form. She was beginning to look the part again. So that at least was one positive to come from the game. One positive, but still far too many negatives.

In the clubhouse afterwards, however, Marwen were to be given a bonus. Two bonuses in fact. Clive was talking to Colin Wilson about the game and remarked on the performances of Bill Sefton and Trevor Denton. Colin agreed that the two were very able cricketers and would probably do well if they played in the League. Indeed, he had tried to get them to play for his team, but they had no interest in playing on a regular basis. They felt that League cricket was too serious and didn't want that sort of tension every week. So in spite of their undoubted ability, the only cricket they played was for the Police team in friendlies.

Clive spoke to T.G. about this and the chairman immediately set about trying to persuade the two to play for Marwen. He must have been quite desperate to have them because he even bought them both a drink. He asked them to consider playing for just the two remaining games this season, then they could judge for themselves how they felt about it. And they'd be doing Marwen a very good turn. Clive came over to join them and emphasised how desperate Marwen's situation was. He told them there'd be no pressure at all on them. If they failed, no blame could be attached to them because the damage had already been done, but if they succeeded they could provide Marwen with a chance of avoiding the drop.

In the end, both Bill and Trevor agreed to play. T.G. bought them another drink. Clive made a mental note of the date. This was one to rank alongside 1066.

So, the friendly game with the police had been beneficial after all. Marwen had found two players who could well improve their chances in the final two matches. In view of the fact that the two were policemen, it could be said that this help had come "out of the blue".

Chapter 12

RAMLEY V MARWEN, ROUND 2

The committee met on Thursday to select the team for Saturday's local derby against Ramley. They had never left it this late before, but with the situation being so precarious they felt they should explore all possibilities before making a final decision. That was why the game with the police had been arranged and selection postponed until after that game. An unusual procedure, but this was an unusual situation. Defeat on Saturday would almost certainly send Marwen down.

The committee members agreed that the extra game had proved most worthwhile, though not for the reasons they had expected. The existing team hadn't played well, so it would have done nothing to boost their confidence. But the game had thrown up possibilities for strengthening the team. The decision to include both Bill and Trevor for Saturday's game was unanimous. Bill could strengthen the early batting, while Trevor could replace Steve Williams, whose bowling (and batting) this season had been nowhere near the standard of which he was capable.

The decision as to who to drop to make way for Bill was also a straightforward one. Ian Cowling's confidence at present was rock bottom. His batting and fielding had gone to pieces and he would probably be only too glad to have the pressure taken off him.

The only other question was whether or not to bring back Jessica. Carl hadn't done well since his recall, so he could make way for her. But Saturday's match would be a high-pressure one, being not only a local derby against their arch rivals but also a match that could seal Marwen's fate, and one committee member was most hesitant about exposing Jessica to such pressure. That member was Jessica's father.

Clive was quite happy about including her. "In cricketing terms, it might make her," he said.

"Or break her," T.G. added immediately. As he had at the start of the season, T.G. was arguing against the inclusion of his daughter, but this time it was for a different reason. He was worried that if she cracked under the pressure on Saturday it might have a serious effect on her.

Clive, however, wanted her in the team. "It won't break her, T.G. She's her father's daughter."

"It's not the right game to bring her back for. Perhaps next week."

"It might be too late then." Clive looked directly at T.G. "You've got to look at this as the club chairman, T.G, not as Jessica's father." He paused, then delivered the decisive blow. "Answer me this. Who can do more for the team's chances on Saturday—Jessica or Carl?"

T.G. knew the answer immediately. There was silence as the others waited for him to speak. He tried to think of a counter-argument. As Jessica's father he could think of a number of them; as chairman of the club he could think of none. "Alright," he said, "I'm convinced."

The decision was made. Jessica would come into the team in place of Carl. The committee was certain that it had chosen the strongest possible team for the most crucial match of the season. The team, as put up on the notice board, read: Clive Walters (capt.), Pete Richards, Bill Sefton, Gary Hudson, Barry Roberts, Kevin Williams, John Price, Arthur Howells (wk.), Trevor Denton, Andy Jones, Jessica Bevan. Reserves: Carl Thomas, Steve Williams.

* * *

On Saturday at 12.45 p.m. the players set off for Ramley in five cars. Bill and Trevor, although they had hitherto argued against the serious nature of League cricket, found themselves relishing the prospect of taking part in such an important match. Neither was worried about being able to cope. What they weren't happy about was having Gary in the car with them. He had insisted on going with his "good mates".

Jessica too was looking forward to the game. Time and again T.G. had told her not to worry about the pressures, but to go out and play her normal game. Jessica hadn't even considered the pressures until her father kept going on about them. But she wasn't going to let such things worry her and by the Saturday morning the roles had been reversed, with Jessica telling her father not to worry about the pressures.

Kevin wasn't looking forward to the game. Ramley was the last place on earth he wanted to go at present. He had heard during the week that Catherine had gone back to her husband and this, of course, meant that it was quite likely she'd be at the game. To be on the safe side, Kevin took his own car, in case he needed a quick getaway. Bob went with him, but wouldn't be returning with him as Carol would be picking him up at Ramley later on.

Clive was looking forward to the game and he wasn't. By this evening it could be that Marwen would be on the way to Division Three. Or it could be that relegation might yet be avoided. Today's game would determine which it was to be. Pat drove the car to Ramley, with Clive and T.G. silent passengers. Hardly a word was spoken throughout the journey. The two men merely looked out, pondering the possibilities.

* * *

The morning had been cloudy at first but had then brightened up. By the time the match started, however, more clouds had appeared. Neither side wanted this particular match to be rained off. Ramley didn't want Marwen getting off the hook courtesy of the weather again, while Marwen couldn't afford to miss out on this opportunity to pick up points and close the gap between themselves and Penford, the team above them in the table.

Stuart Wilkins won the toss and put Marwen in to bat. He didn't want them batting second and playing out for a draw again, especially with the possibility of rain. No, Ramley would get Marwen out as quickly as they could and then they would know exactly what target they were chasing.

Bill and Pete opened the batting and were as solid as rocks as they set about providing a sound foundation for Marwen's innings. Wilkins and Horton, the Ramley opening bowlers, tried all ways to find a way through, but neither batsman looked like getting out, so the Ramley captain took himself off and brought on Ricky James, the off-spinner. This made no difference. The batsmen were still looking good and the 50 came up in the thirteenth over.

The next over was a maiden, the first of the innings. Being more used to playing twenty-over games, Bill decided it was now time to push the score along, especially as no runs had come from the last over. He hit the first ball of James's next over for two. Then on the second delivery he stepped out to drive the ball but misjudged the flight and was stumped. He had scored 31.

It's often the case that when a good partnership is broken, the dismissal of one of the partners is soon followed by that of the other. And that's exactly what happened now. In the following over Pete was caught behind for 21.

Gary and Barry were together again—and again they didn't let the side down. Boundaries flowed from both bats and the second and third batting points were secured. These two had batted well together a number of times this season, yet had never put together a century partnership. That looked as if it would be rectified today—until the run-out.

They had put on 91 runs when Barry played the off-spinner into the mid-wicket area. It was far enough away from the fielder for a single to be taken. At least that's what Barry thought. He called for the run and set off. Gary thought differently and sent him back. Barry slipped as he turned and that cost him his wicket. He scampered back but was a metre short when the bails came off. The Australian had done it again.

A Good Catch

Barry turned to Gary and shouted, "Can't you run?"

Gary replied, "If I could run I'd be in the Olympics, not playing in this lousy League."

Barry glared at him, then walked off. He had scored 38 but knew that it could—and should—have been more.

Kevin was the next player to try not to be run out by the Australian. As the new batsman made his way to the wicket, Stuart Wilkins went over to speak to Gary. "Listen here, pal, I want you to do me a favour." Gary was listening, so Wilkins went on. "I'll be bringing myself on at the other end next over and I'd like to have a full over against our young friend here. If you can manage that, I'll see you alright in the bar afterwards."

"With pleasure," Gary replied.

Kevin was quite surprised to see that all the fielders were well away from the bat for a new batsman. There was a single to be had almost anywhere. He took a single off the first delivery and then Gary played out the rest of the over without even looking for one run. Kevin thought this was strange, especially as Gary was well set at the crease by now. Then he thought that his batting partner must be trying to ensure that there'd be no chance of a collapse.

Wilkins brought himself on as he had said and Kevin looked forward to crossing swords with the Ramley captain. But what followed was far more dangerous than crossing swords.

Kevin played the first ball towards the fine-leg area. There was nobody down there, so it was a chase for the fielder at square-leg. There were three easy runs here, but after the second run Gary called out, "Leave it at two." Kevin couldn't understand it. There were three runs there, no problem. What was the Australian playing at?

He soon found out. The next ball flew past his head. He got out of the way just in time. The next two deliveries were, without doubt, aimed at the body, but Kevin managed to get his bat in the way on both occasions.

The fifth ball went the same way as the first. Again three certain runs. Again the Australian refused to run the third. This time Gary ran well past the stumps on the second run to make sure there wouldn't be a third.

The final ball of the over was another dangerous one, heading for Kevin's eyes until he ducked out of the way.

After the umpire signalled the end of the over, Kevin went down to the other end. Waving his bat under Gary's nose, he told him, "You pull another stunt like that and I'll ram this down your throat. Next time I call, you run. Or else!"

As Kevin turned to walk back, he noticed Stuart Wilkins beaming from ear to ear. This was someone else he wanted to sort out. And he'd sort him out with the bat too. In Wilkins's next over, Kevin was again the batsman. He had already decided that attack was the best form of defence. He guessed that there'd be a bouncer or two coming his way, but he was more prepared now. Actually there were two bouncers in the first three deliveries—and both were hooked for four.

By now the umpire could see what was going on and he warned Wilkins about dangerous bowling. That upset the bowler's plans. Kevin decided to upset them even more. He went down the wicket to the next delivery and drove the ball over the bowler's head for four.

Wilkins was furious. But in his temper he lost control over his bowling and Kevin drove the next ball through mid-wicket for four. Kevin played forward to the last ball of the over and shouted down to Wilkins, "Good ball, bowler." Wilkins was seething.

Sixteen runs had come off the over and while Wilkins would dearly like to bowl at Kevin again he knew that he couldn't because the main task was to win the game. He took himself off for the second time in the match and didn't bowl again that day.

As it turned out the change of bowling brought success. Horton was brought back to bowl and in his first over he had Kevin l.b.w. for 25. Two overs later Gary was caught at mid-off for 57. Marwen were 179 for 5 with eight overs remaining.

Clive and Jessica were now at the crease and neither had yet scored. Jessica hoped she'd do well today and she was not to be disappointed. She and Clive put on another 48 runs, picking up a fifth batting point on the way.

A Good Catch

After fifty overs Marwen had scored 227 for 5, with Clive 24 not out and Jessica 22 not out. Jessica was well pleased. T.G. was also pleased that it had gone so well for his daughter. Even Gary was impressed.

Clive was happy with the situation. He looked up at the sky. Not a cloud in sight. The game was there to be won. It was now up to the bowlers–and the fielders.

* * *

During the interval the teams sat apart in the clubhouse with no mingling between them. Both sides desperately wanted to win and didn't want to show any indication of goodwill to the opposition. There'd be plenty of time for that after the match.

The umpires had stayed outside to talk for a while and when they came in, one of them called over to the Ramley captain, "Stu! Do you want your sweater back or not?" He held up the sweater for Wilkins to see. He had taken it off while he was bowling and hadn't bothered taking it back afterwards.

"Leave it there," Wilkins said, pointing to a chair near the door and the umpire did as requested.

Both teams went back to their various conversations. Apart from Kevin. Having just been given a second cup of tea, he told the others he was going outside to drink it as it was too stuffy inside. A few minutes later he brought back the empty cup. Had there been time, he'd have had a third cup. Seeing as he hadn't touched a drop of the second.

Stuart Wilkins again forgot his sweater on the way out, so he didn't find out until much later about the large stain on it.

* * *

Today Clive decided to revert to a more normal opening attack, giving Andy the first over. In that over he hit the batsman on the shoulder with one delivery, then with the next ball had a loud l.b.w. appeal turned down.

After that some of the Ramley members started to jeer the

young bowler. Almost every delivery brought some comment from them and when Andy was fielding at long-leg during Trevor Denton's overs he was subjected to further abuse, this time at closer quarters.

Clive noticed what was going on and knew what those people were doing. They were trying to break Andy's concentration and impair his bowling. Before Andy's third over the captain had a word with him. "I'll move you away from long-leg next over," he told him.

"No way," the youngster told him. "That would be playing into their hands. They'd think they'd won. And I don't want Ramley winning anything today. Not a thing."

"Are you sure you'll be OK?" Clive asked.

"Just you watch," came the confident reply.

The third ball of the over knocked back the batsman's off-stump. Andy had made his point. He was certainly bowling better today than he had for a long time. Perhaps the barracking was doing him some good.

When he was down at long-leg in the next over, Andy still had to put up with comments from the 'Ramley Kop', but he continued to ignore them. Clive had warned him not to get involved and he fully intended to follow that advice. But he couldn't resist turning towards baiters and smiling after Trevor had taken two wickets in three balls to leave Ramley struggling on 12 for 3.

As in the first meeting between the two sides, Ramley were in deep trouble early on and, as in that first game, they looked to their captain to pull them out of it. He had gone in at No. 6 in that game, but today he went in at No. 5. He took his time getting off the mark, his main priority being to stop the slide which was taking place. He had been out in the middle for five overs before scoring but then, after settling down, he started to score freely. He and Dennis Burrows took the score on to 44 with sixteen overs gone.

Clive now decided to bring the spinners into the attack. Trevor and Andy had done a good job, but a change was needed before the current batsmen became too comfortable. Clive opted for a double change, thinking that this would be more likely to unsettle the batsmen. They would have to cope with two new styles of bowling immediately instead of being able to adapt to them one at a time.

Wilkins wasn't bothered about the bowling changes. He had taken Marwen apart before and was confident that he could do so again today. But there were two important factors present in today's game that hadn't been present in the previous contest. The first was Gary, the second was an ability on the part of the Marwen players to catch the ball.

Both these factors combined to send Wilkins back to the changing room in Gary's third over. He had been struggling against Gary's bowling and had found it very difficult to score off it. In the leg-spinner's third over he tried to drive the ball towards mid-on, but the ball turned sharply, with the result that it went in the direction of mid-off. It didn't get up very much, but enough for Jessica to run in and take a good catch.

In the next over Burrows tried to hit John over mid-wicket, but Kevin took a superb catch above his head. Ramley were 53 for 5 and there were 28 overs left in which to take the remaining wickets.

Gary took two more wickets in his next two overs, one a smart catch behind the wicket by Arthur and the other a good running catch on the mid-wicket boundary by Barry.

Clive was amazed at the standard of the fielding. Delighted, but amazed. The team hadn't fielded like this in a very, very long time.

And there was more to come. Ramley were obviously playing for a draw. Indeed, that was all they could do. The eighth-wicket pair blocked everything and did a good job for their team, using up over after over and taking runs only when there was no risk whatsoever.

By the 35th over the score had reached 69 for 7. The best Ramley could hope for in terms of points was a second batting point if they could get the score up to 80. But they weren't going to hurry about that. They had fifteen overs left, so there was plenty of time. And if they didn't get the second batting point, it wouldn't matter, as long as they didn't lose the game.

Gary had tried everything. He had tossed the ball up high, he had bowled it through quickly. The response was always the same—a defensive stroke just to keep the ball out.

The 35th over was going the same way as so many others had gone before. Then with the fifth ball, the batsman came forward to block it, but the ball clipped the inside edge of the bat and went to Kevin at backward short-leg. The quick-thinking fielder immediately threw the ball at the stumps. The batsman's back leg had strayed out of the crease for an instant. But that was enough, for it was in that instant that the ball hit the stumps—with the back leg out of the crease. Now that back leg and the rest of the batsman's body were on their way back to the changing room.

Ramley, with only two wickets in hand, had to survive 14.1 overs if they were to avoid defeat. They weren't thinking now about the second batting point. The ninth-wicket pair of Mark Johnson and Ricky James had been in similar situations many times before. They were two of Ramley's most experienced players and knew exactly what was expected of them.

Over after over went by with no sign of a wicket. Clive brought Trevor back instead of Gary, then switched Gary to the other end. But still there was no breakthrough. Then for the 46th over he brought Andy back. Still no luck. He tried Pete for the 47th over. No luck.

The 48th over was Andy's. He tried and tried to get some lift out of the wicket, but to no avail—until the last ball of the over. This one did lift and move away, catching the outside edge of Johnson's bat and giving John a catch at slip.

One wicket left to get, two overs left in which to get it. The crowd was enthralled.

Gary came back for the 49th over, but Ricky James played it out comfortably.

Now for the last over. Bill Horton, the Ramley opening bowler, was facing Andy. Clive brought all the fielders in. Ramley had scored only 74. Perhaps the batsmen might take a risk or two in order to reach 80. Perhaps six inches of snow might fall in Tenerife in mid-summer. Perhaps someone might cycle to the moon.

Horton had been told by his captain to forget about scoring runs. What he had to do was be there undefeated at the end of the 50th over.

The first two deliveries were outside off-stump and the batsman allowed them to go through harmlessly. Clive ran over to Andy and told him he must make the batsman play the ball.

Andy was also getting some advice from the barrackers in the crowd again, but such was his concentration now that he couldn't even hear them.

The third ball pitched in line with the off-stump and cut back, hitting Horton on the pad. The Marwen players all appealed, but in vain. The ball had cut back too sharply and would have missed leg stick.

The fourth ball also cut in towards the batsman. It also hit Horton on the pad. But this time it had first caught the inside edge of the bat. Barry, at forward short-leg, dived forward and caught it. The players appealed and looked at the umpire. They were sure that the ball hadn't touched the ground before Barry caught it. But did the umpire see it that way? After what seemed an eternity, the umpire raised his finger. It was all over. Marwen had won.

The Marwen players, as one, jumped in the air. Then they ran around, hugging each other and patting each other on the back. Had they just won a Wembley Cup Final with a goal in the last minute, the excitement wouldn't have been greater.

* * *

The singing and cheering in the changing room afterwards reflected the mood of the team. Jessica had gone with the others into the changing room and had shared in the singing and joking that had gone on. Then when some of the men started to change, she got up and went to the door.

"Where are you going, Jess?" shouted John. "You're one of

us now."

With a serious look on her face, Jessica looked around at the other players and, shaking her head, said slowly, "Oh, I do hope not." Everyone burst into laughter.

"Why the hurry, Jess?" Arthur asked.

"You lot singing I can put up with, your socks humming I cannot." She went out quickly as some of the others started to throw their socks at her.

A few minutes later T.G. rushed in with the news that Penford had only drawn their match with Cernig. The difference between Marwen and Penford had now been cut to only two points. Again the cheers rang out and the singing restarted.

Through all this Clive sat quietly, thinking over what had happened. The other male members of the team undressed, went for a shower and came back, but Clive just sat there. He reflected on how close the team had been to losing out on their objective. One over fewer and the match would have been drawn. Clive shuddered at the thought. But it hadn't been one over fewer. Yes, it had taken fifty overs to take the ten Ramley wickets—but they had had fifty overs in which to take them, so all was well. However close they had come to missing out, the fact remained that the record books would show that Marwen had won and had picked up 22 points in so doing.

Clive was proud of the way his players had stuck to their task. He was proud of the way Andy hadn't given in to the barracking of the crowd. He was proud of the way Jessica had put her previous setbacks behind her. And the fielding? Yes, he was proud of them all for their fielding. All the chances had been taken. Not one dropped catch. When was the last time that had happened?

So they were still in with a chance of avoiding the drop. The difference was two points. Only two points. They could ensure their place in the Second Division by winning their final League match of the season next week—at home to Tresarn. They couldn't miss out now. Could they?

While Clive had been mulling all these things over in his mind, Arthur had finished showering and changing. The wicket-keeper had let the captain sit quietly, realising that the skipper needed time to unwind after the pressures of today's game. But now he thought it was time to snap him out of it. "Are you coming for a drink, Clive?"

Clive looked at Arthur, at first blankly, then with some recognition as his mind returned to the present. "What?" he asked.

"I asked if you were coming for a drink."

"Oh! Yes, yes, of course." Clive got up, picked up his kit-bag and moved towards the door.

"Shouldn't you shower and change first?" Arthur asked.

Clive looked down and realised now that he was still wearing his cricket gear. He laughed, as did everyone else who saw it.

"It's OK, Clive," Arthur said. "We all understand. It must have come as a terrific shock to you."

"Oh, I knew all along we could win," the captain said.

"That's not what I meant," the wicket-keeper replied. "I'm talking about you scoring 24 not out. No wonder you're still in shock."

Clive laughed again. "Another comment like that, Arthur, and I'll put you back in the shower."

"You can't do that," Arthur told him. "I've changed." Then he smiled, "But you haven't."

The other players took Arthur's hint and Clive's whites were given a premature wash—with Clive still in them.

* * *

With all the euphoria following the game, Kevin had quite forgotten about Catherine. But as he walked to his car to put his kit-bag in it, he noticed her Mini Cooper in the car park. So she had come after all.

After depositing the bag in the Lotus, Kevin made his way to the clubhouse. He wasn't looking forward to this. He couldn't fall back on Bob's support, because Bob had already gone. Carol had seen to that. It was all that Bob could do to keep Carol at the ground until the last wicket had gone down. But once that wicket had fallen, Bob had had to move.

Kevin went into the clubhouse and walked straight to the bar, where Barry was already buying a drink for him. The two of them then went to join the others. As he sat down, Kevin noticed Catherine sitting next to her husband at another table.

The evening went along pleasantly enough and Kevin stayed with the Marwen players. The only time he left them was to go to the bar or to the toilet. There were always plenty of people at the bar, so he'd be safe there. And even Catherine would draw the line at going into the 'Gents'.

She did not, however, draw the line at staying in the small corridor leading to the 'Gents', this being the corridor that also led to the 'Ladies'. When Kevin came out after paying a visit, Catherine was waiting for him. "I must speak to you, Kev," she told him.

"No, Cath," he said firmly. "Leave me alone. It's over."

"I know, I know. But I still want to talk."

"There's nothing to talk about. And anyway, you're back with your husband now. I hope things work out better for you this time."

"There's no chance of that. I've got no intention of staying with that pleb."

"I'm sorry to hear that. Now if you'll excuse me." Kevin started to move away.

"Please, Kev," she pleaded. "Can't we meet just once?"

Kevin shook his head. "There's no point."

"In that case I'm . . ."

As had happened on a previous occasion, Catherine had to leave a sentence unfinished because of Jessica. Marwen's female player had just come out of the 'Ladies'. "Oh, Kev, there was no need for you to wait there. I said I'd meet you by the car." She took him by the arm. "Goodbye, Mrs Wilkins," she said as she led Kevin away.

Catherine didn't follow them. She couldn't really, because it would have meant following them through the crowded bar, where everyone would have seen what was going on. That's what

A Good Catch

Jessica was counting on. But, not wishing to take any chances, she led Kevin straight through and out to the car park. The drink that was waiting for him on the table would have to be left. But Kevin didn't mind. He was glad to get away.

They ran to his car, laughing as they went. As he drove away from the ground, Kevin said, "Thanks, Jess. Again. I don't know what I'd do without you."

"Is that a proposal?" she asked.

"Pardon?"

"Never mind."

They sat quietly for a while, then Jessica broke the silence. "Do you realise I've had to leave a thoroughly good gin and tonic because of you and your problems?"

Kevin started to apologise, but Jessica cut him short. "It's not an apology I want. It's compensation." Kevin was confused now. Jessica went on. "Well, the least you can do now is take me somewhere else and buy me another gin and tonic to replace it."

"Yes ... OK ... I'll do that." Kevin drove on, still somewhat perplexed. He hadn't seen Jessica like this before. Fancy making so much fuss about a gin and tonic!

Of course, Jessica wasn't really annoyed about losing the gin and tonic. After all, she had already drunk six. But she wasn't going to miss this chance of getting Kevin to buy her a seventh.

He took her to the same pub he and Bob had been to earlier in the week and bought her a replacement gin and tonic–plus three more which she demanded as her reward. He himself stuck to orange juice. He had learnt his lesson after his last trip to that pub.

After downing her reward Jessica fell asleep in the pub. Kevin had to wake her up before leading her out to the car and taking her home. Once in the car she fell asleep again, an even deeper sleep this time. So when they reached her home, Kevin had to carry her to the door. Fortunately, T.G. had come back early, so he opened the door when he heard them coming.

"One daughter, slightly the worse for drink," Kevin said.

"I was wondering what had happened to her," T.G. said. "That's why I came back early, in case something was wrong."

"No, there's nothing wrong, T.G. She's just been celebrating, that's all. She's certainly knocked back a few tonight." Kevin carried Jessica into the living room and put her down on the sofa.

"Thanks for bringing her back, Kev," T.G. said. "I hope she didn't spoil your evening too much."

"On the contrary, T.G. It was because of her that my evening wasn't spoilt."

T.G. fetched a bottle of whisky from a nearby cupboard. "Have a drink, Kev. We can finish off the celebrations here."

"No, I'd better not. I'm driving. I've had one close shave this week as it is."

"Oh, forget about driving," the chairman said, pouring a generous measure of whisky into a glass. "You can leave your car here and walk home. It's close enough. Anyway, with a few of these inside you, you'll be able to fly home."

Kevin didn't need much persuading. It was indeed a time for celebration.

"And I'll have a gin and tonic," said a weak voice from the sofa.

Chapter 13

NOW OR NEVER

The three of them woke about the same time and were coming to terms with the fact that they were still in the land of the living. T.G., Jessica and Kevin had slept in the chairman's living room, T.G. in his favourite chair, Jessica on the sofa and Kevin on the floor. Not one of them had had a comfortable night, but they had been too drunk to care about that. An empty bottle of whisky lay alongside Kevin on the floor.

Kevin was leaning on his left arm and using his right hand to try and ease the discomfort he was feeling in his neck. But that was only part of the trouble. He wished he could get both hands on the micro-being who was using a hammer to wreak havoc inside his head. Though what he would do to that micro-being was nothing compared to what he'd do to the swine who had put a stick of gelignite inside his stomach and detonated it. Kevin felt ill, really ill.

The other two weren't much better. Jessica made a determined effort to try to speak. "Anyone for breakfast?" she asked.

The two men nearly threw up at the very thought of it. Kevin shook his head, which served only to increase the activity of the hammer-wielding micro-being. T.G. closed his eyes and said nothing.

Five minutes went by and no-one said a word. Jessica got up from the sofa and went over to the window. Kevin was very impressed with that. He might try to walk himself later–say, tomorrow. Jessica drew back the curtains and nearly blinded the other two. She then went into the kitchen to make some coffee. Black, of course.

A few minutes later she brought the coffee into the living room. T.G. had gone back to sleep in his chair. While the decibel level of the snoring increased, Jessica and Kevin sat at the table in the living room to drink their coffee. There was still a reluctance–or was it an inability–to speak.

Again it was Jessica who broke the silence. Well, relative silence, given the snoring. "Thanks for bringing me home, Kev. I hope I wasn't any trouble."

"No problem," said Kevin, proud that he had managed such a long sentence.

"I hope I didn't do anything to embarrass you. I don't remember much of what happened."

Kevin now tried for some even longer sentences. "You were OK. Apart from some rambling."

"Rambling? About what?"

"Asking if I'd propose to you or something daft like that."

"Oh," was the first response. Then Jessica frowned. "What do you mean, 'daft'?"

"Well, marriage ... Us two ... " He sniggered.

"Yes?"

"Come on, Jess. Can you imagine it?"

"Yes, I can," she said, emphasising each word. Then she got up and stormed out of the room and slammed the door behind her. That was a mistake. Now there was a micro-being hammering inside her head. But that was nothing compared to Kevin's state. His micro-being had laid down the hammer and was now using a pneumatic drill instead.

* * *

On Monday evening the committee had no hesitation in naming an unchanged team for the last League fixture of the season, at home to Tresarn. Only one question was raised. T.G. asked,

"Should we order some champagne?"

"That might be tempting providence," Clive warned.

"Rubbish!" the chairman retorted. "You saw how we played last Saturday. There's no reason why we can't have a repeat performance next Saturday."

Clive again advised caution. "Remember the trouncing they gave us in Tresarn. That's no cause for confidence."

"We're a different team now. Ask Ramley."

Glyn agreed with Clive. "There are so many things that could go wrong," the secretary warned. "It might rain. We might have a player injured again. Remember we lost Bob in that first game. Then there's the possibility..."

"Stop!" shouted T.G., slamming his fist on the table. Glyn complied immediately, as did his heart almost. "We've come too far to let it slip now," T.G. said. "If we... When we avoid relegation, we'll have something to celebrate. And we'll do it in style. If by any chance we do miss out on Saturday, then we'll need to drown our sorrows. And we'll do that in style. I'll bring the champagne."

"That's very kind of you, T.G.," Clive said.

The chairman looked at the captain. "I hadn't finished. I'll bring the champagne and the money can come out of the clubhouse funds. Is that agreed?"

There was no point arguing further.

* * *

The week passed quickly for the players. All thoughts were on Saturday's match. Could they pull off a miraculous escape after all that had happened this season? They needed to bridge a gap of two points. Just two points.

On Friday it looked as if they might not get a chance to bridge the gap. It rained all day. Clive listened to the weather forecast after the six o' clock news. For Saturday the weather-man forecast rain in the north but dry conditions in the south. Clive went to the window and looked at the rain. "That bloke must be Australian," he told Pat. "He's looking at everything upside down.

It's probably dry in the north."

"He's giving the forecast for tomorrow, not today," Pat said. "It might clear overnight."

By eight o' clock the rain had indeed stopped. Perhaps the weather-man—and Pat—could be right after all.

* * *

They were right. Saturday morning was bright and sunny. The continuous sunshine dried out the field and the game was in no danger. Only the result was in doubt.

Tresarn won the toss and chose to bat first. Before taking to the field, Clive had all his players in the changing room with the door closed. "I've never been one for giving pre-match pep talks," he said, "and there's no need to start now. You don't need me to tell you how important this game is. All I ask for is full concentration from start to finish." He opened the door. "We go out and do our best. No-one can ask for more."

The team took to the field, raring to go and eager to see wickets tumbling. But it was a long time before any wicket tumbled. The Tresarn openers had taken Marwen's bowling apart in the first meeting between the sides and shared a century partnership. They had done so with the help of some poor fielding by the Marwen players. This time the fielding was much better, but the batsmen still took charge. Halfway through the allotted number of overs, the score was 108 for no wicket. Clive had tried each of his four main bowlers, but not one of them looked like breaking through.

The situation was looking bleak for Marwen. Clive remembered how Pete had come on in the first game and taken a wicket, so he brought him on again today—and again he took a wicket. Ben Titley, one of Tresarn's openers, drove the fifth ball of Pete's first over back down the wicket. He hit it hard off the middle of the bat and the ball flew towards Pete's midriff. The bowler said afterwards that he had to catch it in his hands because otherwise it would have gone straight through him.

That breakthrough was vital for Marwen. It had looked as though the Tresarn openers were going to put the match—and the avoidance of relegation—well beyond the reach of the home side. At least now Marwen had a chance of hauling themselves back into the game. There was still a long way to go, a very long way, but the first step had been taken.

Steps 2 and 3 soon followed as John Price picked up two wickets at the other end, one stumped and the other l.b.w. The stumping victim was the other opening batsman.

Clive took Pete off now, feeling that with two new batsmen in, it would be better to let a front-line bowler have a go at them. He brought back Trevor and his decision was justified by two wickets in Trevor's next four overs. The bowler was working up quite a pace and both dismissals were the result of the batsman being beaten and losing the middle stump.

Marwen's position was looking much better than it had earlier. Tresarn were 134 for 5 and the batsmen were struggling.

However, the sixth-wicket pair eventually came to terms with the bowling and saw Tresarn through to their fourth batting point and well on their way to the fifth. With five overs to go, the score was 182 for 5.

Gary had been brought back to replace a tiring Trevor. The leg-spinner had already bowled two overs in this spell without unduly worrying the batsmen. It was with the third ball of his third over that the chance for a breakthrough came. The ball caught the top end of the bat and flew up in the air to silly mid-off—or to where silly mid-off would have been had there been a silly mid-off. Jessica came running in from mid-off and dived forward, as she had done with success in previous games. But this time she wasn't successful. The ball touched the ground before she got her hands to it.

Jessica asked Clive if she could stay forward. Gary also wanted her there, so Clive acceded to their wishes. Which was just as well, because if he hadn't Marwen wouldn't have claimed the sixth Tresarn wicket with the last ball of the over.

The same batsman who had survived Jessica's attempt to remove him earlier in the over now succumbed to Jessica's fielding, though she herself knew little about it. He drove the ball hard in her direction. She quickly took evasive action, covering her head and turning. The ball struck her back and went up into the air to give Gary the easiest of tasks in catching it.

Jessica was on the floor, not having seen what had happened. The others ran to her.

"Are you alright, Jess?" Clive asked.

"Is he out?"

"Yes."

"Then I'm alright."

She got up and received the congratulations of her team-mates just as if she had taken the catch herself. Her back was sore, but she was content to carry on fielding, even to stay close to the wicket.

"I'll move you away if you like," Clive said. "You can swap places with Kevin."

"No, it's OK," Jessica replied. Kevin heaved a sigh of relief.

With the first ball of Gary's next over, the 48th over, another wicket was taken. The batsman played forward, but the ball turned and caught the top edge of the bat, giving Jessica an easy catch at silly mid-off.

Gary was now on a hat-trick, so Clive brought all the fielders into close catching positions. But the bowler spoilt his chance of making a bit of history by bowling a full toss and the new batsman promptly sent the ball to the mid-wicket boundary. Gary was furious with himself.

The fielders returned to their previous positions and Gary continued with the over. He had the batsman out with the fifth ball of the over–caught and bowled. Why couldn't he have done that three deliveries earlier?

Still, Marwen had taken two more wickets in the over and Tresarn were 188 for 8 with just two overs left. It was an interesting situation. Marwen needed the last two wickets for a fifth bowling point, while Tresarn needed twelve runs for a fifth batting point.

The ninth-wicket pair showed their intentions. They had evidently decided to run everything in an effort to pick up the extra point. They took a single off each of the first four deliveries

A Good Catch

of Andy's final over.

When the fifth ball was bowled, the batsman just dropped his bat on it and started to run, as did his batting partner. The ball had moved forward only slightly. The non-striking batsman ran for the far crease, Andy ran for the ball. The bowler kicked the ball towards the stumps and it hit them before the batsman reached safety. "Owzthat!" Or was it "Goal!"? He was out anyway.

The last batsman came in and hit the last ball of the over for two runs. So Tresarn went into the final over at 194 for 9. They needed six runs to get the extra point, so six singles would do it.

This, of course, was based on the assumption that the batsman wouldn't edge a catch to the wicket-keeper off the first ball of the over. The assumption did not hold, the catch did. Tresarn were all out for 194.

The Marwen players came off the field well satisfied with their performance. Considering that at one stage Tresarn had been 108 for no wicket, to get them all out for 194 was a remarkable achievement.

As they had their tea, they heard that Penford had dismissed Plasmawr for 92, so they too had picked up five bowling points. What was even more disappointing was that Penford now needed only 93 runs to win. That made it imperative that Marwen reach their target of 195. Their fate would be decided by the last innings of the season.

* * *

The innings started well for the home team. They needed to score at about four runs an over and with nine overs gone they were 36 for no wicket. Bill and Pete looked set to provide Marwen with the sound start they needed for this most vital innings.

In the ninth over, however, Pete played back when he should have gone forward and he was trapped l.b.w. for 19.

Gary came in and attacked the bowling from the outset. In no time at all he had passed Bill's score, the opening batsman being content to stay there and leave the more accomplished Australian take the bowling apart.

Tresarn changed to spin at one end, but it made no difference to Gary. The off-spinner's first over resulted in twelve runs being added to the score. It seemed to be going well for Marwen. Gary looked to be at the top of his form. Even his running between the wickets couldn't be faulted. It seemed as if this particular flaw in his play had been removed.

It only seemed that way, however. Bill was on 22 when he played the ball into the covers to the left of the fielder there. Gary yelled at Bill to run and was already well on his way to the 'danger end' if a throw came in. But the left-handed fielder quickly picked up the ball and threw it to the bowler's end. Bill was out by a long way. The Australian had done it again.

Barry came in but had to wait until the next over to face his first delivery. That over was bowled by the off-spinner and Barry attacked his bowling from the outset, as Gary had done. He drove the first ball straight through a gap in the off-side for four. He drove the next ball straight into the bowler's hands. Things weren't going so well for Marwen now. But at least Gary was still there.

They couldn't say that after the next over. He was l.b.w. for 35. Marwen were up against it at 86 for 4 after twenty overs. They were up with the required run rate but had lost four of their main batsmen in the process.

Clive joined Kevin and the pair took to the task of stabilising the innings. They didn't take any chances but still moved the score along in good time. They added 29 runs in their first eight overs together, but then things started to go wrong. The Tresarn off-spinner was switched to the other end and the change did him good because he started to pin the batsmen down, bowling two maidens in a row. Also one of the opening bowlers had been brought back and the batsmen found it difficult to get him away too.

Six runs came in six overs. This wasn't good enough. Kevin decided to try to break the grip the bowlers were exerting on the batsmen. He tried to drive the off-spinner over the fielder at mid-off, but succeeded only in driving the ball straight to the fielder at mid-off. Kevin was out for 16 and Marwen were 121 for 5, still

A Good Catch

74 runs short of their target.

Jessica came in and Clive told her to take her time. She did. Clive didn't. He was out in the next over, caught behind when trying to effect a square cut. He had scored 20. The scoreboard showed 121 for 6.

Trevor Denton came in and scored three runs off the last ball of the over. This took him to the other end to face the off-spinner. Bill told Clive that Trevor didn't like facing spin bowlers. This just added to Clive's worries.

The worries eased as Trevor comfortably stroked the first ball through mid-wicket for two. Then the worries increased as Trevor tried to do the same to the next ball and was bowled. 126 for 7. Sixty-nine runs were still needed, and this from batsmen who, apart from Jessica, had done nothing with the bat all season.

But everyone has to start somewhere and John started his batting season in this game. He and Jessica played sensibly, taking singles where they could, hitting out only at bad deliveries and always running the first run quickly to improve their chances of having a second. The score moved on past 150, then past 160 to secure the fourth batting point. Only one target was left now—195. Could these two do it?

No, they couldn't. John was bowled for 23, leaving Marwen on 164 with just two wickets left and seven overs to go.

Arthur went in. At his age—he would be 51 in November—he wouldn't be able to run too many quick singles, so he and Jessica had to ensure that any runs taken could be run comfortably. Not that Arthur was too happy with that even. His running days were long gone. But Marwen's overs were nearly gone too, so Arthur did his best. He ran and ran and the score moved on to 180. There were three overs to go and by now both the opening bowlers were on, trying to win the game for Tresarn.

Arthur wondered whether they would reach the target before he had his coronary. He hit the first ball of the next over for two. Which put the team that much closer to victory and Arthur that much closer to his coronary. He was nearly run out on the second run. He had to run faster than ever to get back safely, He just managed it. But that was it as far as running was concerned. He couldn't go on like this.

He took his time to recover, then faced the next ball. He allowed it to go through. He didn't have the strength to hit it anyway.

"Come on, Arthur," shouted Gary from the boundary. "Get on with it."

"I will if you get me another pair of lungs," Arthur tried to yell back in annoyance. He should have kept quiet. The yelling put even more strain on him and he started coughing. When the coughing stopped, he faced up to the next ball, which he cut for four runs.

"Well done, Arthur," shouted some of his team-mates.

"Well done, Arthur," the wicket-keeper told himself. He had now found a good way of avoiding running. He promptly cut the next ball for four as well.

With the score on 190, there were only five runs to get. But Arthur wouldn't be getting them. He was l.b.w. to the next ball. He had scored 17 runs and taken his team to within sight of victory. It was now left to Jessica and Andy to see them home.

Andy faced up to the last ball of the over. He played it on to the off side and they ran a comfortable single. The Marwen players watching from the boundary wondered whether it had been wise to take the single, because it now kept Jessica from facing the bowling. Still, the runs had to come from somewhere and that single took them to within four runs of victory. One good stroke away from victory.

Unfortunately, they were to get no closer. The Tresarn bowler really dug in the first ball of the penultimate over and the ball came up sharply. Instead of moving out of the way, Andy used his bat to, as he saw it, protect himself. The ball went off the edge of the bat through to second slip, thereby justifying the Tresarn captain's decision to keep two slips during those last overs even though the game was so close.

Marwen were all out for 191, with Jessica 21 not out. She went over to Andy immediately. He was nearly in tears. "I'm sorry, Jess," he said. "I should have left it."

"Don't worry about it," she said. "It was a very good ball. The best one he bowled in the time I was out there."

Andy shook his head dejectedly. "It's all my fault, I shouldn't have taken that single. I should have let you face the bowling."

"I ran the single too," she told him. "We had to take the runs as they came. Anyway, I could have gone out myself to that ball. Then we'd be saying we should have run the single when we had the chance. So forget it. It's only a game."

"How can I forget it?" he shouted. "We're down now and it's my fault." There were tears in his eyes as he spoke.

Jessica put her arm around him as they started to walk off. "Hey, come on now. You can't take all the blame yourself. You've got to share it with the rest of us. We didn't get relegated because of one ball."

* * *

The rest of the Marwen team stood despondent on the boundary. Gary muttered, "I said it was stupid to take that single."

Clive turned on him. "I don't want to hear any more comments like that. Right? Just shut up." The captain left the others and went on to the field. Firstly, he went to shake hands with Keith Owen, the Tresarn skipper. "Well played, Keith," he said.

"Sorry about the result," the other captain said, knowing what the defeat meant for Marwen. "Still, it was a terrific game. You can be well proud of your team."

"That I am, Keith." said Clive, starting to move away. "I'll see you in the clubhouse afterwards." He went over to Andy. Seeing how upset the youngster was, Clive stood in front of him, blocking his path. "Listen, young man, I don't want tears from any of my team after a performance like that. And if you're thinking of blaming yourself, forget it. If we're down, we're all to blame, not just you. OK?"

"I've been telling him that," Jessica said.

"What do you mean, 'If we're down'?" Andrew said. "Of course we're down. We all know that."

Clive shook his head. "Penford may have lost too."

Andrew sniggered. "Fat chance!" He brushed past his captain, then went straight past the others and into the changing room. He didn't want to talk to anybody and he didn't want anybody talking to him.

"Is there any news from Penford?" Jessica asked.

"Nothing," Clive replied. "We haven't heard anything since tea. Just can't get through. We've tried phoning and phoning. No luck."

"I expect they won," said Jessica, hoping to be contradicted.

Clive nodded. "Probably. Still, we gave them a good run for their money." He put his arm around her. "And as for you, my girl, I shall look forward to having you in the team next season, whichever division we're in."

"Thanks, skip," Jessica said and they went to join the others.

* * *

Understandably, the Marwen changing room was quiet. Yes, they had come very close to pulling it off. But very close wasn't good enough. Word was going round that Penford had won their game by four wickets and had therefore saved themselves.

Clive wasn't going to allow the players to wallow in their misery. He got up and said, "OK, you lot, cheer up. It's not the end of the world. If we're in the Third Division next year..."

Barry interrupted. "Drop the 'if', skip. We all know we're down."

Clive spoke firmly. "No, we don't know we're down. All we've heard is a rumour. We haven't had confirmation. But if that's the way you want it, OK. So we're down. But only for a season. Other teams have bounced back straight away. So can we Especially the way we've played the last couple of games. So get your heads up. If it's Division Three next year, so be it. But it'll be Division Two the year after. OK?"

As Clive had been talking, Bob had come in. He closed the door behind him and stood to one side to listen to the captain. After Clive had finished, Bob said, "Sorry, Clive, but I for one have no intention of playing in the Third Division. No way."

Clive was taken aback by Bob's statement. Bob had been so loyal to the team in the past. "But it'll only be for one season, Bob. Surely, you'd stand by us for that."

Bob shook his head. "No, not even one season. The Third Division isn't for me."

Clive didn't know what to say. Neither did any of the others.

"And another thing," Bob said. "As soon as some of the others have had time to think things through, they won't want to play in the Third next year either."

Now the others did speak. "Not me." "We're not all traitors, Bob." "Loyalty still counts with some people." Clive again had cause to feel proud of his team.

Bob let them have their say, then spoke again. "Yeah, yeah, you're all having a go at me now. But feelings are still raw after what's happened. But you wait. Wait till you've had time to take everything in. Then you'll change your minds." The others yelled their disapproval, but Bob raised his voice too. "And I'll tell you why..." They tried to drown him out, but he persisted. "I'll tell you why you'll change your minds. We've just heard that Penford were all out for 57. We're still in the Second. It's official."

The players, as one, let out a loud yell, though not one of disapproval this time. This was followed by cheering and singing for some time after. The noise could be heard by the Tresarn players in the changing room next door. Ben Titley turned to his captain and said, "I thought it was us who won."

* * *

It wasn't long before T.G. came into the home team's changing room with a magnum of champagne. Glyn James and Doc followed with paper cups. The champagne was gone in no time. But this was only the start. The celebrations had a long way to go yet.

When the players started going to the showers, Bob went out to the car park, where Carol had come to pick him up. She was sitting in her gleaming red Micra, of which she was so proud. As

Bob approached, she made a point of looking at her watch.

"Something wrong with your watch?" Bob asked.

"No, but obviously there's something wrong with yours. I've been waiting here for over ten minutes."

"Oh ... Er ... Sorry about that, babe. It's just that we've been celebrating."

"I see. So they managed to win their precious game then."

"No, they lost."

Carol looked questioningly at Bob. He got into the car and explained. After the explanation he said, "There's going to be a terrific night here tonight. Why don't we stay and join in the celebrations?"

"No thank you, Robert. I would prefer a quiet evening, just the two of us."

"But we can have a quiet evening any time. Tonight is something special for the club. Don't you see? We've just avoided relegation. There'll be a party atmosphere here."

"I don't feel like going to a party tonight, thank you."

Bob opened the car door. "Well, I do. You do what you like, Carol. I'm staying."

"Robert!"

"No, Carol. I'm sorry, but this is important. You've got to realise that cricket is important to me. This club is important to me. It's a special occasion here tonight and I mean to be a part of it."

"Is the club more important to you than me?"

"You know it isn't. And if you avoided relegation, I'd celebrate with you too." Carol didn't laugh. Bob got out of the car, then asked, "Are you coming?" Still Carol said nothing, so Bob walked off.

Soon after, he heard a car door slamming. "Wait for me," Carol shouted. When she caught up with him she kissed him and said, "If it's that important to you, then I suppose it's important to me too."

They walked arm-in-arm towards the clubhouse. "And as you're celebrating," Carol said, "you can break open your wallet and buy me a glass or two of champagne. I'll leave the car here tonight. And if they haven't got champagne, I'll have something equally expensive."

Bob asked, "Are you sure you want to stay?"

* * *

After the celebrations in the clubhouse had been going on for about an hour, T.G. got to his feet and, banging a tray on the table, called for silence. "As chairman of the club," he said, "I think I should make some sort of speech on this important day for Marwen Cricket Club." Everyone groaned, but T.G. went on. "It'll be a short speech." Everyone cheered.

"This season hasn't been one of our best by a long way," the chairman said. "We've had plenty of problems, but I'll have more to say about those in my speech at the Annual Dinner." More groans. "What I want to say now is that we can all be proud of the way we've fought back over the past few weeks and pulled ourselves out of a seemingly hopeless situation. I always knew we could do it." Louder groans this time. "But now I'd like to thank all the players and their captain for their fine efforts in keeping Marwen in the Second Division."

The applause was loud and long. T.G. took the hint and sat down. He motioned to Clive to get up and say something. The captain duly obliged. There were no groans this time, only cheers.

Clive cleared his throat. "I only want to say a few words." Louder cheers. "Like T.G., I'm very proud of our players and the way they've pulled together to help avoid relegation. I don't intend naming individuals. We've done this as a team. So what I'd like to do is thank *all* our players for their efforts." More cheering. "I'd also like to thank the players of Plasmawr for their efforts today." Loud cheers again. "And finally I'd like to thank the chairman for his kind words—and for his offer to buy a drink for all the players."

Cheers and whistles rang around the clubhouse again. The players were amazed that T.G. had made such a gesture. It was so unlike him. T.G. was amazed too. He hadn't said a word about buying drinks. But Clive had forced him into a corner.

Clive smiled at the chairman. He was surprised to see the chairman smile back. What did T.G. have up his sleeve now?

A few minutes later T.G. brought a pint of lager over to where the players were sitting. He put it down on the table. "There you are. Your captain told you I was buying a drink for all the players. Well, there it is."

"Where's the rest?" Arthur asked.

"Here you are," the chairman replied. "Eleven straws. Enjoy." He put the straws on the table.

Everyone burst into laughter. Clive knew now why T.G. had been smiling. Clive kept his eyes fixed on the chairman, who was doing his best to avert the captain's gaze. In the end he did look over. Clive raised an eyebrow. T.G. said, "Alright, alright. I'll go and get the drinks." More cheers from the players.

* * *

Just before the speeches had started, Kevin had moved round to sit next to Jessica. They chatted for a while, then listened to the speeches. By now Kevin had finished his pint and Jessica had nearly finished her gin and tonic. "Let me get you another drink," Kevin said. "Gin and tonic?"

"Oh no, Kev," she replied immediately. "I've already had two. I'll have an orange juice."

"Orange juice? You can't have orange juice. We're celebrating."

"I know. But I don't want you or anybody else having to carry me home tonight. I caused enough bother last week."

"I didn't mind."

"Didn't you?"

"No. In fact, I had a good time."

A look of realisation came to Jessica's face. "Oh yes, of course. The whisky in the house afterwards."

"No," Kevin said instantly. "Well, yes, I did enjoy the whisky. But I enjoyed the company as well."

"Dad had to replenish his stocks after that. He bought two more bottles yesterday and put them away in the cupboard." Jessica now mimicked her father's voice. "I'll put them in here in

A Good Catch

case young Kevin calls again."

Kevin's face lit up. He picked up his glass and moved off. "I'll get you a gin and tonic."

Jessica smiled as Kevin went to the bar. She thought to herself, "I hope Dad's remembered to get some whisky in."

Chapter 14

A GOOD BASH

With the League fixtures over, there were only two events left in Marwen Cricket Club's calendar for this year: the annual match against a touring team from the Midlands and the club's annual dinner. The former was to take place on the Thursday following the final League match, the latter on the second Friday in October at a hotel just outside Swansea.

Marwen wanted to field their strongest side for the tour match against Heathwood, as the visitors had trounced them last year by over 150 runs after the home side had put out a weaker side than usual. This year Marwen wanted revenge, so if possible would name the same side that played against Tresarn. Unfortunately, neither John nor Barry could get time off from their work, so two changes had to be made. Steve Williams and Ian Cowling were brought in to replace the two unavailable players.

Heathwood batted first. Andy and Trevor opened the bowling and made a good job of it, taking two wickets apiece in the first fifteen overs. Three of these wickets were catches, so the recent improvement in the fielding was continuing. Kevin had been tried again in the slips and he held two catches there, one straightforward and the other an excellent diving catch which he held with an outstretched right hand.

With Heathwood on 47 for 4, Marwen were in a strong position. But after another fifteen overs the score was 147 for 4 and the position was looking very different. John Steadman and Dave Keane had batted extremely well to bring about this change.

A Good Catch

Clive had varied the bowling to try to get a breakthrough. He was hampered to some extent in that he didn't have an off-spinner, but he made full use of the variations he did have at his disposal. He tried Gary at both ends in turn, but the batsmen found the Australian's bowling to their liking and hit him all over the place. His six overs to date had cost 44 runs and he hadn't looked like getting a wicket.

The breakthrough came in the 31st over, but it had nothing to do with the bowling. The ball was hit square on the leg side and Andy came running round from long leg for it. The batsmen had run the first run quickly in order to try for the second. Andy too had run quickly and was quite near the ball when they started their second run. If they were banking on a misfield they were to be disappointed. Andy picked up the ball cleanly and threw it in. He couldn't have placed his throw any better. It went straight to Arthur, standing over the stumps, and when Arthur took off the bails Steadman was still two strides short of the crease. It had been a foolish call on Keane's part to go for the second run, but Marwen weren't complaining. Steadman was.

The score moved on towards and past the 200 mark. By now Clive had resorted to Pete Richards again. Pete's first two overs had been very expensive, yielding 17 runs, but Clive decided to try him for one more over. Some of the others doubted the wisdom of this, but a caught-and-bowled in that third over fully justified the captain's decision.

That was the beginning of the end for Heathwood. Andy took a further two wickets and Trevor, having been brought back instead of Pete, took the other two. Steve had again come out of a game with no wickets to his name. He was glad the cricket season was over. He'd be playing rugby through the winter and would think seriously about whether to bother with cricket again next year.

Heathwood were all out for 224, leaving Marwen with a big target for victory. They started very well, with Bill and Pete putting on 51 for the first wicket. But then both openers were dismissed in the space of two overs. Bill was bowled for 23, then in the next over Pete was l.b.w., also for 23.

After that Marwen produced another of its famous collapses, Gary was out for 4, Clive for 2 and Ian for 8. At 72 for 5 things were looking bleak for the home side. Like Steve, Ian was glad that the season was over.

Jessica joined Kevin and they got down well to their task of improving Marwen's position. It was now that a disease with which Marwen were all too familiar made another appearance on the village ground, but at least this time it was affecting the opposition rather than the home team. The Heathwood players started dropping catches. Kevin was dropped three times and Jessica twice. Two of the chances were put down by the same player, Paul Hickson, and he had the misfortune of putting another down later on. The ball seemed to be following him around. Ian Cowling knew exactly how he felt.

Not that the two Marwen batsmen–or batspersons–were complaining. They were quite happy to continue their chase for runs. Both Kevin and Jessica produced some fine strokes and ran well between the wickets–which was a far cry from the way the running had gone the first time they had batted together. The 50 partnership came up in even time and Jessica had scored 22 of those runs, including three boundaries. She then tried to drive a fourth boundary, but didn't get her foot to the pitch of the ball and presented mid-off with the simplest of chances.

When the fielder, Jack Cartwright, took the catch, his teammates yelled with delight, so relieved were they that a catch had at last been held. They ran over to congratulate him as if he had pulled off the catch of the season.

At 122 for 6, Marwen were still over a hundred short of their target. A disillusioned Steve walked on to the field and three overs later an even more disillusioned Steve walked off the field, having scored only seven runs. He used to go in at No. 3, but he now he felt he should go in at No. 12.

Kevin was 38 not out and looked set for a half-century unless he ran out of partners. Trevor (nine runs) stayed with him for a short while and Arthur (four runs) an even shorter while. Not

A Good Catch

that anyone could blame Arthur. He still hadn't recovered from Saturday's batting performance.

By now Kevin was 45 not out and Andy came in to join him. It was an off-spinner who was bowling and there was one ball left of the over. Andy played the ball and there was an easy single in it. But he didn't want it. He had learnt his lesson on Saturday. Kevin could keep the bowling to try for his fifty.

Kevin hit the second ball of the next over through mid-wicket for four runs and the third ball past mid-on for two. He had got his fifty and he milked the applause that came from his teammates on the boundary. But try as he did, he couldn't manage a single off any of the remaining deliveries to get him down to the other end.

So Andrew had to face an over from the off-spinner. And what an eventful over it was. The young batsman was completely devoid of confidence in his batting, so he played tentatively at the first ball. The ball went up in the air towards Paul Hickson at mid-on. The fielder had to run in for the catch, but just as he was getting to the ball he stumbled. He got his hands to the ball as he fell forward, but when he hit the ground the ball came out of his hands. Andy had survived.

The next ball was bowled and Andy started to come forward, then went back. The ball hit him on the pad and the fielders appealed. But the umpire didn't give him out. Andy had survived again.

By now he had had enough. He was going to be out anyway, so he might as well fling his bat at everything. The strokes weren't particularly elegant and wouldn't be found in any coaching manual. But they were effective and produced three successive boundaries, as most of the fielders had by now been brought in.

Andy was more confident now and went down the wicket to hit boundary number four. This time the stroke was quite majestic, but he missed the ball and was stumped. Marwen were all out for 168, with Kevin not out 51.

* * *

Clive waited on the boundary as the players left the field. He went to the Heathwood captain, Don Prince, and congratulated him on his victory.

"Thanks very much, Clive," was the other's reply. "It was a fair performance overall, I suppose. Apart from the fielding, that is. Did you see all those dropped catches? I wish my lot could catch as well as yours."

Clive nodded without saying a word. If only he knew.

* * *

In the clubhouse afterwards the beer flowed freely. Early on in the session Don Prince got to his feet and called for silence. He made a short speech, in which he thanked the Marwen club for its hospitality, the ladies for the tea and the players for a good game. He then moved on to the presentation of awards.

"And now for the Heathwood awards," he announced and everyone cheered. "Firstly, of course, there's the Rubber Duck Award for the Heathwood player who comes out of the game with a duck. There are two nominees this year, Ken Simpson and myself." More cheering. "But as I survived four balls and Ken only two, I have no hesitation in awarding the Heathwood Rubber Duck to Ken."

There was applause and cheering as Ken moved forward to accept the award. It was a rubber duck hanging from a ribbon and this was hung around Ken's neck. He would have to wear that for the remainder of the evening. There was more cheering as he returned to his seat.

"Next," said the Heathwood captain, "comes the Poor Fisherman Award for the player who can't catch anything. This award has been well earned today by a man who, if we had come by train, would probably still be in Heathwood. He wouldn't have caught that either. So come on down, Paul Hickson."

A very embarrassed Paul Hickson went over to the captain to the sound of cheering from everyone else present (apart from Ian Cowling who was ever so glad that Marwen didn't have such an award). The Heathwood players were cheering loudly but they were only too glad that it was Paul, not they, who was getting the award. Paul was presented with a miniature bucket on a ribbon and would have to wear that around his neck for the rest of the evening.

Don Prince continued with the awards. "And now for the Jogger's Award, presented to anyone who enjoys running so much that he's prepared to run other players out in order to indulge his own delight." More cheers. "This award goes to none other than Dave Keane and I call on John Steadman, the man he ran out, to make the presentation."

Dave and John moved to where their captain was standing. John took the pair of running shoes which Don gave him and hung these around Dave's neck.

As the two players returned to their seats, Arthur leaned over to Gary and said, "If we'd given you a pair of those every time you ran somebody out, you could have opened a shoe shop." Gary was not amused.

Don Prince went on. "And finally to a more serious presentation. I have with me a plate with the Heathwood emblem on it and I call on Clive, Marwen's skipper, to come forward and receive this plate, which we are presenting to the Marwen club as a token of our appreciation. Of course, if we had lost, we'd have taken it back with us." Everyone laughed.

Clive went forward to receive the plate. Don stepped away from the table to meet him. He held out the plate, but before Clive's hand could grasp it, Don let the plate fall to the floor. It smashed into pieces.

Don looked at Clive, who was acutely embarrassed. The initial reaction of the other people was to laugh, then they quietened down, feeling sorry for the Marwen skipper. Don said aloud, "I thought you lot didn't drop anything."

Clive was blushing profusely by now. Then Don put his arm round his shoulder. "Sorry about that, old man. I dropped it deliberately. That wasn't the proper plate. Here's the proper one." He took another plate from a bag beneath his chair and gave it to Clive. The Marwen captain held on to it tightly with both hands.

By now everyone was laughing.

Clive made a brief speech. He said he had had too much of a shock to say more. Then Don officially closed the awards ceremony and everyone got down to the serious business of enjoying themselves. This they did well into the night and many of them spent the following morning regretting it.

* * *

Marwen Cricket Club's Annual Dinner was always held on the second Friday in October, so everyone at the club kept that particular evening clear each year. Gary Hudson had left the village the week after the Heathwood game and had gone to visit various people in Scotland, the north of England and Norfolk. He had also spent a few days in London, though he still didn't see his friends there. They were never in when he called. He couldn't understand it.

He made sure he was back in Marwen in time for the Dinner. He had arrived on the Thursday and was again staying with Pat and Clive. He would go back to London over the weekend, stay for a few days and then fly back to Australia.

A coach went from Marwen to the Preswylfa Hotel, some fifteen miles away, and most of the people going to the Dinner went in that. A few cars went too, one being Jessica's. She hadn't been feeling well and took the car in case she'd need to leave early. T.G. chose to go on the coach instead of with Jessica. She had also offered Kevin the chance of a lift and he had accepted. That was one of the reasons T.G. chose the coach. Two's company...

* * *

After a three-course meal, including a turkey dinner, T.G. rose to make his speech. "Well, ladies and gentlemen, it now falls to me, as chairman, to undertake the task of reviewing the season." He coughed before continuing. "It was a season of problems and there were many, many problems. But everyone stuck to their tasks and it all came right in the end. We survived. Only just,

A Good Catch

mind you. But we survived. And we'll be playing in the Second Division again next year." The players cheered.

T.G. waited for the cheering to subside before continuing. "We had a disastrous start to the season, our play was a joke. The situation was so serious that a change of captain was called for by some people, whoever they were." Everyone groaned.

"But Clive stuck to his task, and I, for one, am glad he did." Now there was loud applause as well as more cheering. "Clive stood by his players and said all along that things would come right in the end, as they did. But I wish they hadn't cut it so fine." Some laughter.

"Then we lost Bob before the half-way stage. He managed to break his arm while fielding. I'm wondering whether there's any truth in the rumour that he did that deliberately so that nobody could attach blame to him if the team went down. Still, I'm glad that his arm is much better now and, according to Carol, is being put to good use." More laughter and cheering–but not from Carol, who was quite embarrassed.

"We needed to replace Bob with somebody good. But instead we had to make do with an import from Australia." More laughter. "Seriously though, Gary came into the side and gave us the lift we needed. His bowling and batting were great assets in our fight to stave off relegation. He kept the players on their toes. Especially those batting with him, as they knew he'd do his best to run them out." Cheers came from the Marwen players, other than Gary

"Then for the last two games we had some help from the police. Bill and Trevor came into the side and played their part in helping us to safety. No wonder American tourists think our police are wonderful.

"And while on the subject of Bill and Trevor, I'd like to ask the rest of you to keep buying them drinks tonight so that later on, when they're less sober, we can try to persuade them to come back and play for us next season." Applause and cheers again.

"Of course, I've left out one other newcomer who played an important part in our battle for survival, someone called . . . " He made a point of looking down at a piece of paper in front of him. "... Jessica Bevan." Louder cheers. "Her hardest task of the season was getting into the side, because apparently someone on the committee was stubbornly refusing to allow a woman into the team." The audience groaned loudly.

"But she persevered, got into the side and proved that committee man wrong. She had her setbacks, but she overcame them. Setting aside the fact that she's my daughter, I'd like to say that she showed a courage, determination and strength of character of which she can be proud." Loud applause broke out and when it died down T.G. added, "Those are qualities she must have got from her mother.

"There are many who will remember the season well for one reason or another. There are some things we'll all remember: Clive trying to head the ball, Arthur trying to run himself into the ground, Gary trying to run everyone else into the ground.

"Then, of course, there were the dropped catches. I had thought of listing them, but some of us have to be in work on Monday." He looked around the room as he added emphatically. "That is one aspect of our play which I hope will not return next season."

T.G. took a sip of whisky before continuing. "There are players I haven't mentioned, players who got on with things in their own way but who all played a part in keeping us up. I'd like to thank all the players, without exception, for their efforts over the season and I look forward to seeing you make a much greater impact on the Second Division next season." More cheering.

"I'd like to thank the ladies for the way they kept us all well fed during the season. In particular I should mention Pat, who made sure that everything ran smoothly again." T.G. paused while the audience expressed their appreciation in a loud burst of applause and cheers. "I hope the ladies are happy with the new boiler–though I still think there was plenty of life left in the old one." There were loud groans now, particularly from the women involved in making the teas.

"I should add that the quality of the food for the Brynteg game was exceptionally high. So high in fact that there was even

A Good Catch

talk of the men taking over the work permanently."

"You're welcome to it," Pat shouted out.

"But we knew how much you ladies enjoyed making the food, so we decided against it." More groans.

"Finally I'd like to thank the committee members for their work throughout the season. They've helped to keep the club running smoothly off the field and for that I'm sure we're all grateful." Loud applause broke out again.

T.G. took some more whisky while the applause went on. He was glad he was coming to the end of his speech as his glass was almost empty.

"You may have noticed that we don't have a guest speaker here this evening to say a few words and present the awards. There are two reasons for this. The first is that nobody could really follow one of my speeches." Loud groans again. "The second, and more important, reason is that we felt we wanted to honour one of our longest-serving members. I refer, of course, to Donald Owen Cooper. Doc to all of us here.

"I was talking to Doc the other week and he happened to mention that he'd been with the club for forty years. So I thought–and the other committee members agreed with me–that we should let Doc have the honour of presenting this year's awards in recognition of his services to the club.

"There was another reason though. He promised not to make a long speech, which meant I'd be able to replenish my glass that much quicker. My glass is almost empty now, so I'll call on Doc to say a few words and then make the presentations."

T.G. sat down, but Doc didn't get up for a while. The applause following T.G.'s speech went on for some time. When it finally died down, Doc got up and everyone started applauding again.

He kept to his word about not making a long speech. He started by saying how much Marwen Cricket Club meant to him and compared the club now with how it had been when he first joined. He spoke of T.G.'s playing days and got a big laugh when he said, "And I can assure you that T.G. played then far better than he umpires now."

He then spoke briefly about this last season, concentrating mainly on the changes that had been seen: a woman playing in the team for the first time; an Australian in the team for the first time; and the police represented in the side for the first time in over twenty years.

Then came the awards. Doc mentioned that the Young Player of the Year was Hugh Bowen, but the presentation to him would be made at a special evening in the clubhouse for the youth team in a week's time. The Second XI Player of the Year was Tony Mears, who happened to live next door to Doc. As Doc said, "This was the nearest I could get to taking a trophy home myself."

Now the time had come to announce Marwen's Player of the Year. It was widely reckoned to be a two-horse race between Kevin and Gary. Gary was the favourite following the great impact he had made on the side, but Kevin had in his favour that he was a home-grown player and had played the full season, one of the few players to have played in every game.

Doc made the announcement. "Marwen Cricket Club's Player of the Year is ... " He paused for effect. " ... Gary Hudson."

Everyone applauded, including Kevin, and the Australian went up to receive the trophy. But it wasn't long before people started thinking that the wrong decision had been made.

Gary accepted the trophy, then turned to face the bulk of the guests and made his acceptance speech. "I'd like to thank you for this award, though I must say I'm not surprised by it. I think I deserve it and I'm sure the rest of the team would agree with that."

People didn't know whether he was joking or not, but they were soon to see that he wasn't.

"When I came here, the team was in an absolute mess. It needed something–or someone–special to sort things out. Although in the end it was close, I'm glad I succeeded and this award shows that you share my feelings about this.

"I've had a good time in Marwen. If I might say so, the people in the village tend perhaps to be rather insular, but in time I came to feel accepted and was glad I came. Having said that, I have found life very quiet here and I'll be glad when I'm back in

A Good Catch

Australia."

Kevin whispered to Jessica, "He's not the only one."

Gary continued. "It'll be good to be back playing proper cricket again with a higher standard of players. Not that I'm saying anything against Marwen. In comparison with other teams around here, you're not bad. Not bad at all. But of course, I have to compare that with the standard I'm used to back in Oz.

"I'd advise the players here to work hard on their fielding and especially their catching. It's something which could cost you dearly in the future if you don't sort it out.

"Anyway, that's next season. What we're concerned with here is last season. As I said, I'm glad I've played here. I thank the players for their support. I thank Pat and Clive for their hospitality. And I thank you all for recognising my contribution by giving me this trophy. Thank you."

He returned to his seat. At first there was complete silence as he went. Then Doc started clapping his hands and a few others followed suit. In the end most of the rest joined in, but there was no warmth in the applause. None of them had heard such a speech before–and didn't want to again.

Doc said that that was the end of the formalities, thanked everyone for giving him the honour of making the presentations and sat down. This time the applause was much louder and longer–and much more sincere.

One other presentation was made. On behalf of the club, T.G. presented an inscribed silver salver to Doc.

* * *

There was no doubt as to the main talking point for some time afterwards. Everyone's opinion of Gary had reached an all-time low.

Yet he still managed to take it even lower. When the dancing started, he came over to where Jessica and Kevin were sitting. He told Kevin, "Hard luck about the trophy, mate. Perhaps you'll win it next year. Seeing as I won't be here."

"For which we'll all be grateful," Kevin said.

Gary ignored the remark and asked Jessica if she'd like to dance. "So that you can say you've danced with a winner tonight and not just losers," he said.

Kevin started to get up from his chair, but Jessica put her hand on his arm. "Leave it, Kev. It's not worth it. I'll have one dance, then I'll be back."

She went with the Australian to the dance floor, they had their one dance, then she started her way back. Gary told her, "When the slower music starts later on, I'll come looking for you."

She turned to face him. "Don't bother, Gary. Seeing as that sort of music is supposed to be suitable for people in love, I suggest that you dance with a mirror." She walked off.

Gary then danced with Pat and while dancing told her that it still wasn't too late for her to give him the sort of going-away present they would both remember for a long time to come. Pat ignored the comment, putting it down to the fact that he'd had a lot to drink already that evening. She didn't tell Clive, knowing that if she did he'd half-kill Gary.

But Pat didn't need to tell Clive. Gary had spoken loudly enough for others on the dance floor to hear. It was Pete who told Clive.

* * *

Later on, Kevin went outside for some air. It was getting very hot inside. It was to get even hotter outside, because when Kevin came out Gary was already out there smoking a cigar. Kevin turned to go back, but Gary saw him and called him over. "Sorry if I offended you in there, mate. I didn't know you and Jess were getting it together."

Kevin said nothing. Gary went on. "She's quite a girl, our Jess."

Now Kevin did speak. "She's not your Jess."

"Oh, I don't know," Gary said. "Given the right circumstances I think Jess and I could..." He didn't get to finish the sentence. Kevin's fist coming into contact with his chin halted the flow of words. The Australian fell backwards to the ground and Kevin jumped on top of him, ready to give this arrogant colonial the lesson he'd been asking for ever since he came to Marwen.

But the lesson didn't get very far before it was stopped. Clive had come out immediately when he heard that Gary and Kevin were talking outside. He knew the two wouldn't remain talking very long. He pulled Kevin off his adversary and told him to go inside.

"Let me finish it," Kevin shouted. "He's been asking for this."

"Pack it in now, Kev," Clive said, "and get yourself back inside. Jess is waiting for you."

Kevin dusted off his clothes and went inside. Gary got up from the ground. There was a trickle of blood coming from his nose, but apart from that he seemed alright.

A few minutes later Clive went back inside and went to the bar. Another minute or so and Gary came in and headed for the men's room. He was looking much the worse for wear. There was blood pouring from his mouth as well as his nose now and he was going to have a real shiner around his left eye.

Kevin watched the Australian go by and was amazed at the state he was in. Then he looked at Clive. The captain was rubbing his right hand–the knuckles were rather sore.

The rest of the evening went smoothly, though there was still a bit of excitement left. At about midnight the music stopped and T.G. went to the microphone. "Excuse me interrupting, but I've got a bit of news you'd probably all like to hear. I don't know which of them is the more drunk, but I've just been told that Bob has at last asked Carol to marry him and she has consented."

Again applause and cheers rang around the room. Everyone was surprised at the news and for some time after the announcement Bob and Carol were surrounded by well-wishers.

Jessica and Kevin were sitting at their table. "And about time too," she told Kevin.

He said, "I only hope Bob doesn't regret it in the morning."

"Oh, don't say that, Kev. Where's your sense of romance?"

Jessica looked at Bob and Carol talking to some of the well-wishers. Then she looked at Kevin. It was time he settled down now. And who better to settle down with than her? She and Kevin had been out together a number of times over the past few weeks and had enjoyed each other's company. It had taken her a long time to get Kevin's attention, but she had at last succeeded and now that she had him, she meant to keep him. The cricket season had been full of dropped catches, but this was one catch Jessica was determined not to let go.

www.ingramcontent.com/pod-product-compliance
Lightning Source LLC
Chambersburg PA
CBHW021100080526
44587CB00010B/319